ROAD
ATLAS

The Rock Dog Gang

Illustrated by Joanna Carey

BRIAN EARNSHAW

The Rock Dog Gang

A Pied Piper Book
Methuen Children's Books

Also by Brian Earnshaw

Dragonfall 5 and the Empty Planet
Dragonfall 5 and the Master Mind
Dragonfall 5 and the Super Horse
Dragonfall 5 and the Haunted World
Starclipper and the Song Wars
Starclipper on the Snowstone
Starclipper and the Galactic Final

First published in 1987
by Methuen Children's Books Ltd
11 New Fetter Lane, London EC4P 4EE

Printed in Great Britain by
St Edmundsbury Press Ltd,
Bury St Edmunds

British Library Cataloguing in Publication Data

Earnshaw, Brian
The rock dog gang. – (A Pied Piper book)
I. Title II. Carey, Joanna
823'.914[J] PZ7

ISBN 0–416–02042–9

Contents

I

A bad place for big dogs

It was a cool late April night in Kingsdown, the old suburb on the hill above Bristol. The wind was from the north-west, blowing over the Severn from Wales. A purple Ford Capri 3.0 litre, M registration, with pale corn coloured seats, drew up in Lilleshall Street outside Beacon House – *Dog Kennels and Boarding, Veterinary Facilities*. At the wheel sat Wayne Taylor, a young man who had got divorced a week ago and was off to Canada to work with computers. Sitting beside him was a large hairy dog, a Bearded Collie called Lucan.

As the car stopped, Wayne put his arm round Lucan's neck.

'I'm sorry, boy,' he said, 'but this is where you go. You know I'd take you with me to Canada if I could, but it's just not on. Mary didn't want you any more than she wanted me. But we've had some good times, haven't we? You and me and the old car.'

Lucan did nothing. He didn't even turn to look at Wayne when he opened Lucan's door and caught hold of the dog's collar.

'Come on, Lucan, you won't be staying here for long. They'll find you a new home, perhaps with some kiddies;

and there'll be a car too. You'll be able to go for trips. Like with me.'

Wayne was very near to crying, and if Lucan had tried to lick him, or jumped, or barked, the tears would probably have come. But the dog just sat there, not looking at him. Lucan was no ordinary dog. He understood everything that Wayne was saying and he had a very good idea exactly what was happening. He was as intelligent as an average human being. So Wayne had to pull him out of the car by his collar and lead him, against the scuffling of his paws, to the door of Beacon House.

Before Wayne could press the door bell, the gate to the entry at the side of the house opened and a woman came out into the light of a street lamp. She was wearing an open overall and smoking a cigarette.

'It's Mr Taylor, is it?' she said. 'You were on the phone this morning.'

'That's right.'

'And this is your dog. Bring him round the side here to my surgery and let's have a look at him.'

Wayne followed her down the entry, stooping to tug Lucan after him. A winding garden fell steeply down into the dark, but they turned into a lighted shed behind the house. There were cases of medical instruments but it smelt of garden twine and fertiliser and stale boiled potatoes.

'You'll be Miss Fran Bosker, I take it?' asked Wayne.

'No, I'm Julie Bosker. Fran Bosker's my sister, she's gone to bed, we run the business together. And this is the young fellah, is it?' she caught hold of the dog's collar and took him from Wayne. 'What's he called?'

'Lucan.'

'Lucan, eh! Come here, boy. He's a fine fellah. A fine fellah, ain't he!'

She patted Lucan hard along his ribs.

'Yes, I'm very fond of him,' Wayne said. 'I wouldn't part with him, but going to Toronto, starting a new job, you know.'

'Toronto! Well, no place for a dog.' Miss Julie Bosker drew hard at her cigarette. 'He'll be better off here, we'll find a good home for him,' she said firmly, a new glint in her eye.

'You think you'll be able to? I wouldn't want to just leave him,' Wayne said. 'He's great company.' Was he doing the right thing, he wondered – this woman looked hard. But he had no choice.

'Dog like this! No trouble at all. We'll find somewhere for him, don't you worry. There's the registration fee, and that's our guarantee, as you might put it.'

'Oh yes. Five pounds, isn't it?' Wayne held out a note which the woman took.

'Seven-fifty for big dogs,' Miss Julie said quickly. 'It's the food they eat. He might be with us for a week before we place him and we like to feed them real meat. Conditions their coats, you know. My sister probably didn't tell you on the phone but don't you worry. Fran and I know dogs from the bark to the biscuit,' Miss Julie laughed, but it turned into a smoker's cough. 'We ought to,' she spluttered on, 'Father was Master of Hunt, you know.'

'Oh yes. Well, I'll be going.' Wayne looked again at the dog, but Lucan looked through him, so he turned and went out. From the road came the sound of a starter wheezing; at the third turn the engine came to life and the car was gone.

Miss Julie clipped a metal lead to Lucan's collar and stood back to look at him. A stout older woman in a camel hair dressing-gown appeared in the doorway.

'Your nightcap's ready, Julie,' she said, then saw Lucan. 'Oh, this is the new one, is it? He looks nice. Will we be able to find him a home?'

'Dog this size? Not a hope!' Miss Julie replied. She drew at her stump of cigarette and blew smoke out. 'Who do they all think they are?' she asked crossly. 'They buy big dogs that cost two pound a week to feed, then dog food goes up so they expect us to find an even bigger sucker to foot the bill. Look at him, Fran! Would you pay three pounds a week to feed a sulky hearth rug like this?' She twitched the lead scornfully.

'Did you get the five pounds?' Fran asked.

'Seven-fifty: conscience money! Knew I'd get it when I saw the guilty look in his eye,' Miss Julie Bosker snorted.

'Trust you, Julie,' said Fran admiringly. 'Anyway, we can keep the dog for a bit with that sort of money.'

'We keep him a week,' her sister retorted firmly, 'in case the owner looks in on us. Then we put him down.'

'Seems a shame.' Fran gave Lucan a sentimental look.

'We're running a business here, not a pets' home. Come on, my lad.' Miss Julie started out into the garden, tugging Lucan after her. 'We'll show you down to your private suite with bathroom and colour T.V. Keep the drinkies warm, Fran, won't be half a mo.'

Lighting her way with a torch she led Lucan down a steep path between apple trees. They passed a row of silent single kennels, each one in its own wire enclosure, then turned left to a gate in a strong wire fence. She unlocked this and pushed Lucan through into a cement floored yard, slammed the gate again quickly and stood for a moment outside, grinding her cigarette butt into the path.

'If you don't like your fellow guests much,' she said, 'don't worry, you won't be seeing them for long.'

Then she climbed back up to the house.

In front of Lucan was a double row of boxes laid one upon the other. In each one a dog was lying awake. From the bottom box on the left came a deep warning growl.

'Fight! Fight!' it said.

With a rustle of straw a large Alsatian stepped out of the box and growled again.

'Fight!'

Lucan's mind turned from the cold beastliness of what Miss Julie had just said to deal with this more immediate trouble.

'All right,' he told himself, 'if anyone has to be made an example of, it might as well be an Alsatian.'

'Long-haired freak, fight or grovel!' the Alsatian challenged.

There was a restless stirring in the shadows of the boxes as other dogs, half-seen, got up to watch the fight.

'Have you torn any children's ears off lately,' Lucan asked insultingly, 'or was it just the usual patches from the postman's trousers?'

The Alsatian rushed forward, stupid with rage, just as Lucan had meant him to be. As the Alsatian lunged, jaws open, trying to grab Lucan's ear, Lucan sidestepped, ducked, and bit a firm hold on the bigger dog's left foreleg, then twisted with the whole weight of his body. The Alsatian toppled heavily on to the floor of the pen, wrenching agonisingly the leg that Lucan was holding. Lucan let go and leaped easily up on top of the double row of boxes.

'Easy go!' he called. 'Let's leave it at that and all go to sleep, shall we?'

'Fight! Fight!' the Alsatian shouted. It limped across and made a clumsy leap to get at Lucan. Using a paw, as no normal dog ever does, Lucan cuffed the Alsatian hard in the eye. It fell back awkwardly and tried to use its right foreleg to brush across its bruised left eye. This put all its weight on the strained left foreleg and the Alsatian yelped miserably, then brought the painful left foreleg up to deal with the swollen left eye. That was even worse. The Alsatian looked up at Lucan, then limped away to a corner of the pen.

'That's all for this evening, folks,' said Lucan. 'I'll have something to say to you in the morning. There's going to be no more violence; I'm not that sort of dog. Now, back to your boxes and your dreams.'

Soon the pen was quiet again. Lucan was left alone up on top of the boxes, staring out at the orange lights of Bristol, below in the valley. For the first time in his life Lucan was having to think hard and plan ahead. He was just beginning to realise how unusual he was and that it was time to start making things happen and not just wait for people to push him around.

Lucan was two years old. He had been born at the breeding kennels at Half Tide Farm on a little tidal inlet between two local atomic power stations. This may have had nothing to do with Lucan's being a completely unusual dog but it is true that his mother, Half Tide Handsome Eileen, and his father, Half Tide Handsome Hrothgar, both loved splashing about in the muddy water of the Severn when they were out for exercise.

So perhaps, and this is only perhaps, there may have been a radiation concentration in the waters there and this might have caused a genetic mutation to Lucan's brain so that he was born with a human intelligence.

Certainly there was nothing to show that he was extraordinary except for a rather higher forehead than Bearded Collies usually have. His coat, blue black with white markings, was thick and he stood well, but because of his forehead the breeder, Mrs Williams, decided not to show him, and sold him to Wayne Taylor for £25.

Dogs are normally very easy-going. It's not quite fair to say that they are stupid because the world they live in never asks them to be clever. They tend to broadcast pictures to each other rather than talk, but ever since Lucan had been about six months old he had been able to understand all the human conversations he had heard around him. No one had ever noticed this and he had still behaved like an average dog. If Wayne Taylor said, 'We'll take the car down and do some shopping in Westbury,' Lucan would get up and make for the outside door. Then Mary Taylor would remark, 'I'm sure that dog understands everything you say.'

But neither Wayne nor Mary realised for a moment that this was exactly true, because though their dog could understand, he couldn't speak. As a result Lucan was very well informed for a dog but he only enjoyed the things that Wayne had been interested in: sport, rock music, driving cars and watching T.V.

Now everything was changed. He had dogs to cope with, not humans, and just a short time to persuade them that they were in deadly danger, and that the old woman who fed them meant to murder them all!

2

A pit for the enemy

Morning came slowly with the grey airs and traffic noise in the main streets down the hill. By six o'clock the other dogs in the pen had begun to stir. Lucan pretended to be asleep, secretly taking everything in, his quarter-open eyes hidden behind his tangled hair.

The first dog to get up was the Afghan. He scrambled out of the box where he had slept so uneasily and hurried round all four wire walls of the pen, bumping his head as if there should be an open gate somewhere. When he found that there was none he shook his tangled coat, looked brightly around the garden and barked.

'Stupid,' thought Lucan, 'like all Afghans, but he means well and he's very young.'

The bark brought a Labrador and a Boxer out from their sleeping places to see what the morning was doing. The Labrador was very pale gold with grey in her coat. She walked carefully out of her box, looking right and left first, as if she expected to see something, then she stood quietly in the centre of the pen.

'Guide dog for the blind,' Lucan decided. 'Must have been bad at her job or she'd never have ended up here.'

The Boxer came tumbling out of sleep, slurped water

from a trough, sniffed the Afghan, nipped the Labrador, kicked the large flat food bowl and spun sideways into a corner, all before you could count up to five.

'A nervous wreck,' Lucan listed him firmly, 'all the common sense bred out of him, not unusual in a Boxer. So anxious to please everyone that he ends up irritating everybody. Easy to see why they got rid of him; he needs firm discipline and definite things to do.'

The Boxer made so much noise and fuss that the other dogs got up. There was the Alsatian, still limping. He ignored the rest and went to sit in the far corner of the pen where he could glare at Lucan and see what he was doing. Then there was a very heavy white clumber spaniel with enormous ears. He got up looking tired and promptly slumped down again just below Lucan, panting as if he had had a hard day in the fields.

'Aye aye, squire!' Lucan thought. 'Take it easy or you might bring on a heart attack. Whoever brought you here must have carried you, because you couldn't have walked.'

The last dog looked like no other dog Lucan had ever seen before, unless it was a large unclipped black poodle. But his head was too firm and characterful to be a poodle's, and no poodle ever grew a coat quite so tightly curled and shining. This dog came bounding springily out of his box, took one look at the other dogs and then began to snuffle in the corner by the gate.

'An open tin of meat here!' He broadcast the picture of the meat so sharply and clearly that the other dogs, even the sulky Alsatian, went scuffling into the corner after him. As Lucan watched them he saw the strange curly dog back out of the scrimmage and stand away from the others, panting cheerfully and slowly wagging his tail. One by one the dogs decided that there was no tin of meat in the corner and turned to look foolishly at the curly dog. His only response was to leap up on to the boxes near Lucan and stand there barking at the awakening city.

'A joker,' thought Lucan, 'and a dog who doesn't care what kind of an effect he has on anyone. I can see why people got tired of him! Now I wonder what I can do for this lot? First of all, how do we get out of here?'

Rather unattractive cooking smells had been blowing down from Beacon House for some time before the two Bosker sisters came out of the surgery and started down the steps to the kennels. Fran Bosker had a watering can in one hand and a big bag of biscuits in the other. Julie Bosker carried a heavy bucket of mash over one arm and a ladling pannikin in one hand; half a cigarette slanted from her mouth. Both sisters wore leather boots to their knees, Julie with jodhpurs and Fran with an old green skirt.

They fed and watered the barking dogs in the separate boarding kennels first. They were only here for the holidays. Then Miss Julie came clanking past a low, brick-built shed to the big dogs' pen.

'Hello,' she said, setting her mash bucket down, 'and how's Death Row this morning?'

Up on the boxes Lucan felt his blood go cold again, but the other dogs just crowded around the gate, tails wagging automatically. Miss Julie unlocked the gate and it opened outwards, but as it swung she blocked the gap squarely with her own body and drove the bucket hard at the dogs' noses to push them back.

'Down, sir! Down!' she shouted, and shut the door behind her quickly. There would be no chance of escape there, unless they could knock her over and trample on her. Lucan noticed her leather boots as she kicked the

Afghan hound out of her way; it would be no use biting those and only an agile Chihuahua would get between them.

'Greedy varmints,' she went on, 'anyone would think you hadn't been fed for a week.'

She sloshed what was left from the bucket into the flat food bowl and stood back. As the six dogs bent eagerly down to eat the mash the Boxer caught a piece of meat which the Alsatian had just spotted. Instantly the Alsatian snarled and bit one of the Boxer's short ears. There was a pitiful wail and the Boxer sprang back from the food bowl to stand uncertainly in the middle of the pen, whining, while the Alsatian ate with furious speed in the space which he had cleared.

Miss Julie turned grimly to Miss Fran, who had come up with her bag of biscuits and her watering can.

'See that, Frannie,' she nodded towards the Alsatian. 'That big beast eats his weight in food every week. What do you think about it?'

She nodded her head again towards the low brick shed along the path.

Miss Fran's face puckered weakly.

'Well,' she said, 'I suppose we might as well. No one's likely to come for an Alsatian after the publicity they've been getting.'

'Right!' Miss Julie looked satisfied. 'No need for you to come in here, old girl. They've still plenty of water and they're too big for biscuit. Chuck the bread over the fence.'

While her sister was throwing three stale loaves into the pen, Miss Julie stepped out carefully backwards.

Lucan thought. Then he looked at the low brick shed. Then he thought even harder.

As Miss Fran made her way back up the steps to the

house, loaded with cans and pails, Miss Julie went into the shed. Hissing, clanking noises came from there for a few minutes, then Miss Julie stepped out wiping her fingers on a piece of rag and looking very satisfied. She began to whistle 'Some enchanted evening, you may see a stranger' as she strode back up to the house.

When the other dogs had finished pushing the food bowl around to get the last scraps, Lucan stood up on top of the boxes and gave one sharp frantic bark for attention. With all the dogs looking at him he began to broadcast mental pictures with all his might.

What he wanted to warn them about was that if they did not escape they would all be dead. Again and again Lucan pictured the low brick shed, then Miss Julie, and then all the dogs lying dead in the shed.

The Afghan hound just thought he was telling them to have a good sleep in the brick shed. The Clumber spaniel got the idea of danger and the shed, but just didn't seem very convinced by the notion. When Lucan showed them open gates and dogs running happily free down roads, they all liked those pictures but just blankly wondered how this was to be managed.

And all the time the Alsatian sneered and scratched the cement floor. Lucan broadcast his warnings until the Afghan and the Boxer stopped attending and began playing a game of nip and chase. Then the Alsatian cut brutally in with a show of mind pictures which said:

'I'm called Victor. Because of your tricks last night I'm lame. When I'm fit again I'm going to take you by the throat and shake you until I feel like dropping you. And listen to this: I'm a guard dog; I'm very important. People use me all over this town because I'm fierce. They feed me on meat, great chunks of it, not the slosh they feed to us in this place. What you say about danger and the brick shed is a load of wind and cat squawking. Soon people are going to come to these two old women and say "We want Victor", and they'll take me and give me meat – whole bowls of it. Now keep quiet! The dogs here were happy before you came.'

Lucan looked at the others. They had all watched Victor's pictures, and understood them. Lucan had lost.

And at that moment Miss Julie Bosker came striding down the steps carrying a big sack. This time none of the dogs pretended to be stupid. They all watched as she came down whistling 'Lady of Spain, I adore you'. First she went into the shed to leave the sack, then she came out with a large raw bone. When she reached the gate of the pen Victor was waiting there – pawing up the gate in his eagerness and snarling warnings to the other dogs to keep back. Miss Julie half-opened the door, took Victor by his collar as he reached for the bone and held the bone ahead of her so that Victor pulled her towards the shed.

'This is what I told you: great chunks of meat,' Victor threw back over his shoulder. 'This is how guard dogs live. They've come for me!'

'Keep thinking with Victor,' Lucan told the other dogs. 'Victor, keep showing us what you can see.'

Victor and Miss Julie disappeared inside the low brick shed. The door slammed behind them. All the dogs in the pen hung desperately on to the picture of the juicy bone which was still leaping from the Alsatian's mind to theirs. 'Meat! Meat!' Victor flung at them from inside the shed. Then a little sound of anger and frustration came with the 'meat' cries, and the picture of the bone seemed further away, perhaps on a bench or table. But next came a picture of a metal container closing around, then darkness and no picture at all, but a sharp scent that caught the back of the throat. Until, in a very short time, there was no picture and no scent, no feeling of a mind at all.

'And that is what death means,' Lucan said. 'Unless we get away from here that shed is where we will all go.'

And this time they believed him.

Miss Julie came out of the shed, tugging at a heavy sack with a loosely-changing shape inside it.

'That's all that's left of Victor,' Lucan told them, 'and that's why we have got to work together and escape. We must dig a tunnel.'

'Dear, dear oh dear!' said the old Labrador.

'You give the orders, boss,' said the curly dog. 'We're right behind you!'

As soon as Miss Julie had gone, the dogs got to work. In the pen there was just one soft patch of earth three clear metres from the gate, and here they began to dig a tunnel. Lucan put the Boxer to work first to calm his nerves. He worked until his paws were raw, then Lucan nipped his docked tail and ordered him to drink and rest.

The Afghan worked at the tunnel next, because he was growing bored already and snapping at flies that were not there. But Afghans on their long elegant legs are not the ideal dog shape for tunnelling, and when Lucan caught him trying to bite soil out of the back of the tunnel instead of scraping it with his front paws, he took him off the rota and set him to sweeping the disturbed soil out through the wire, into the boxes, under the boxes – anywhere where it would not betray them. Lucan took the next shift himself and burrowed forward for half a metre, just about six centimetres below the cement floor, to show them that he was a dog of action. It left him filthy and exhausted, so that all he could do for the next few minutes was try to clean his face with water and then lie back watching the others.

All the time they dug one of the dogs sat up on the top

boxes keeping watch on the house up the hill. When Miss Julie came out to peg clothes or Miss Fran came out to the dustbins everything stopped and one of the dogs lay straddled across the hole of the shaft.

The second feed of the day was at six o'clock. Half an hour before this the Clumber backed awkwardly out of the shaft scuffing soil behind him, and all the dogs set to work, nosing and scuffling and pushing, to hide every last particle of fresh soil from sight. To make sure of the final effect Lucan made the Afghan go around the pen with his head down, flapping his beautiful long ears as a kind of mobile duster. But this was really to punish him for being so unhelpful in the tunnel.

The flat food bowl only just fitted over the mouth of the shaft. Too many large dogs going up and down had worn the tunnel entrance wider than Lucan had originally measured it, so the bowl tilted ever so slightly on one side and it was too late to engineer a prop to support it.

Promptly at six the two Bosker sisters came jangling down the steps. This time Miss Fran was first to reach 'Death Row'.

'There's going to be a lovely sunset,' she declared, leaning against the gate.

'So keep your eyes on it,' thought Lucan, 'and don't look too closely at our food bowl.'

Miss Julie came up in a gust of stale tobacco smoke with the mash pail on her arm.

'Glorious, isn't it, Fran?' she agreed, turning to look at the western sky. 'You know what I always say when I see a sunset?'

'No, Julie, what's that?' Fran asked.

'I always say that if there is a God, then he must be an artist!'

'What a lovely thought, Julie,' said Fran, 'that is a lovely thought!'

'Let's put it like this,' Miss Julie continued, crinkling her eyes against the light, 'when you see a sunset like that you know that this funny old world of ours must have a purpose, don't you?'

'Julie, you're right!' Fran agreed enthusiastically.

'I mean, even these horrible hounds of ours,' Miss Julie gestured towards the pen, 'if I didn't know the beasts better I'd say they'd made a special effort to clean the place out for us this evening. Of course it's just us and Springtime, but I can't see a speck of muck or dirt anywhere.'

Lucan shivered nervously, cursing the Afghan's flopping ears for being such an efficient duster.

'Bless them,' Fran gushed. 'They shall all have some biscuit this evening for a treat.'

'You're too soft-hearted for this game, Fran,' her sister said. 'Father always said "never put an animal lover in charge of animals" and he was right. That's why I make money out of it!'

'Wag your tails but don't jump up at them,' Lucan ordered as Miss Julie unlocked the gate.

'Aw, bless them! Look at them!' said Fran, seeing a half circle of quiet, tail-wagging dogs gathered behind the food bowl. She stepped forward and tipped a stream of hard biscuits into the side of the bowl. It began to tilt over the tunnel shaft. The dogs watched helplessly as it tilted more and more. Two more biscuits and the lot would slip down the hole.

'Tricks!' Lucan broadcast as hard as he could, and, putting his head down, supported by his broad forehead and two forepaws, he made a perfect three point headstand, with his back legs crooked and wiggling very slightly to preserve his balance. Quickly catching the idea, the curly dog sat up on his haunches and held his forepaws up in a 'beseech' attitude.

Fran Bosker stepped back in delight.

'Did you ever see dogs do that before, Julie?' she cried.

'Begging's two a penny, but I never saw one stand on his head before outside of a circus,' Miss Julie replied grudgingly. To cover her crossness at having to praise something, she tipped a pannikin of mash into the empty side of the food bowl. Upside down, Lucan saw the bowl balance safely again. He dropped his legs and stood up.

'Slowly!' he called as the Afghan came blundering cheerfully up to the delicately poised food bowl. With polite bites and careful tongue curls the dogs started on their dinner.

'Something odd going on here today!' said Miss Julie as she filled the water trough.

'They're subdued, poor mites,' Fran told her, 'losing their little friend this morning.'

'One mouth less to feed,' declared her sister breezily as she locked the gate behind her. Slowly, chatting and admiring their vegetable patch, the two climbed up to the house and went in to watch television.

'Good team work,' said Lucan, and it was a measure of what working together under the threat of danger can do that all the other five dogs could understand now what he was saying. They were all learning how to connect with each other. Rolling the food bowl aside Lucan went down for the first shift.

As dusk fell they laboured through the last yard of soil towards the gate, the fence, and freedom. Lucan and the curly dog crawled out for a rest, leaving the Clumber and the Afghan to take their places. Lucan was sore in his paws, his back ached with crouching, his fur was matted with soil, but soon he would be out. He would be running his own affairs, no more owners! These other dogs did not know how to enjoy themselves but he would soon teach them!

He and the curly dog sat side by side on top of the boxes, breathing the cool air in quick pants. There was a light taste of petrol vapour on his tongue: a reminder of the lovely world of cars, roads, movement.

'At this time of night,' Lucan told the other dog, 'before he got married, my owner would take me out in the car, and I'd hang my head out of the window to pick up the rush of air. He always drove in the fast lane.'

'I worked at nights,' the curly dog said, 'but it was great: fetching back birds and hares and all sorts.'

'Where was that?' Lucan asked.

'South somewhere the other side of the river.'

'Were you a gamekeeper's dog?'

'No, a poacher's; more fun but more trouble.'

'What happened to your owner?' Lucan wanted to know.

'Police trouble,' said the other dog. 'He went on the run. I never saw him again. Sad, really.'

'You'll get over it,' Lucan told him firmly. 'What's the name of your breed? I've never seen anything like you.'

'Irish Water Spaniel,' the curly dog said, 'we're hard and lean, and our coats are oily. My name's McKlickety. You can call it quietly on a dark night.'

Lucan was just going to tell his name when sad sounds came pouring out of the tunnel and the three dogs on the digging shift came backing out of the shaft. The Clumber squeezed out last.

'What is it, Squire?' Lucan asked. The Clumber was licking a torn claw on his left forefoot.

'Iron and concrete,' the Clumber replied, and went on licking.

Lucan dived down the tunnel and groped his way to the end. He felt about carefully in the dark. It was as bad as it possibly could be. The tunnel had reached the line of fence just under the gate and it had hit a solid line of thick wire mesh set into concrete. Miss Julie had taken no chances.

In the stuffy darkness he tried to stand upright and hit his head a sharp crack on the thin cement of the pen floor. 'The thin cement of the pen floor,' he thought, and in a moment he knew what to do.

3
P.C. Minster strikes!

There was a light mist next morning in the valley below Kingsdown. It covered the spreading suburbs of the city but left the Somerset hills standing up clear on the other side of the Avon. It was going to be a good day and Miss Julie was full of it. Whistling 'If I were a blackbird' she came briskly up to the big dogs' pen, set her bucket down and peered through the wire as she unlocked the gate. The dogs were all still lying sleepily in their boxes, which was unusual.

'Rise and shine, you lazy rabble!' she shouted. 'Make the most of life; you haven't got much of it left!'

She chuckled, picked up her bucket, stepped into the pen and crashed straight through the thin cement floor into the tunnel beneath.

'Freedom and Liberty!' Lucan shouted. 'Jump over her, dogs, and up the garden path. Keep together!'

As she fell, Miss Julie scraped her shins agonisingly on the edges of the cement; she felt a sharp pain in her right ankle and found herself kneeling in a shallow pit with breakfast mash all over her legs. Her eyes were at ground level and she looked up in time to see a tide of dogs leaping over her and out through the gate which she had left swinging open as she fell. Just one dog was left; the old Labrador, trained always to help humans in distress, responded automatically when she saw Miss Julie floundering in Lucan's cunningly prepared trap. She came to the edge of the pit, whimpered, and gave Miss Julie's face a lick. Miss Julie's reaction was just as automatic.

'Ruddy animal!' she raged, and threw the empty mash bucket at the helpful old dog. It was just what was needed. Gathering her strength, the Labrador jumped over Miss Julie and hurried off up the garden after the others.

Miss Fran Bosker was just locking up a boarding kennel, when she looked down the steps and saw five dogs bounding up towards her.

'Snarl,' Lucan ordered. 'All together, snarl!'

With a breathless 'Oh, no!' Miss Fran skipped back into the kennel and slammed the door, leaving the keys outside and locking herself in with the Borzoi.

The dogs went storming past her up the steps, through the entry, round the side of the house, and on to the road. As the old Labrador padded up after them Miss Fran called out in a quavery voice.

'Julie, Julie, I think the big dogs have gone mad. Are you all right down there?'

'Bust my ankle,' Miss Julie called back. 'Come down and give me a hand, will you, Fran? I've fallen down a drain.'

'Julie, don't be angry, please, but I can't, I've locked myself in.'

Miss Julie gritted her teeth, shut her eyes tightly and called for strength.

'If it's the last thing I do,' she swore, 'I'll get those dogs' pelts and stitch them into a rug to use in the scullery. So help me if I don't.'

Very painfully, using a bean stick as a crutch, she picked her way up the steps, unlocked her sister and sent her ahead into the house to phone the police.

The call from Cotham Police Headquarters came through to Patrol Car 49 at 8.50 hours. Police Constable Terry Lewis should have been at the wheel, he was a Bristolian and he knew the streets backwards, but Police Constable Malcolm Minster was actually driving because he came from Birmingham and thought Bristolians like Terry were too easy-going.

'Call come in from Lilleshall Street from a Miss Bosker,' their radio growled, 'of Beacon House. She says a pack of six large dogs has escaped, and they're fierce. One of them might be mad or all of them might be mad or maybe just this Miss Bosker's mad and the dogs don't exist. Anyway, she sounded agitated so drive round that direction and have a look-see, will you? Over.'

'Will do immediately,' P.C. Minster snapped. 'Over;' and he swung the patrol car briskly away down St Michael's Hill.

'Bosker!' P.C. Lewis groaned. 'The Misses Bosker! Them two witches, they're always in trouble. Any dog that gets out of their clutches deserves a taxi ride to Temple Meads Station, I reckon!'

P.C. Minster pursed his lips and turned the car crisply left into the long rows of disjointed Georgian houses that line the top of Kingsdown. P.C. Minster liked to be addressed as M.M. by his friends, not that he had many, and he was anxious to become a Chief Constable as quickly as possible.

'Mad dogs!' he snapped. 'Pull yourself together, Lewis. Get the old grey matter moving. Could be rabies, anything! This might be the start of an international incident. Keep your eyes skinned and looking ahead.'

P.C. Lewis sighed.

'All right, if you say so, M.M, but we've just passed them down that side street.'

P.C. Minster braked intensely to a halt.

'What side street?' he snarled.

'Patrick Place, one block back, leads down to Sutherland Street,' Terry told him. 'I think it was them, six dogs, looked as if they was having a conference.'

Patrol Car 49 made an edgy three point turn and roared back down the road.

A conference was exactly what the dogs were having.

The first thing Lucan had to do when they rushed up the entry and out into Lilleshall Street was to keep them together. The other dogs were inclined to cock their legs up against walls and jump about expectantly in the sheer pleasure of being out of the narrow pen. The Afghan and the Boxer began to gambol off downhill, simply because that was the easiest direction. Lucan dived after them, nipped both their heels and told them firmly:

'United we stand, divided we end up in the gas chamber like Victor.'

That brought them back smartly. They waited for the old Labrador to come puffing up out of the entry and then all six of them jogged quickly uphill for several streets, turned up Patrick Place, and settled round a lamp post and a row of dustbins put out for clearing from a little mews terrace.

'Right!' said Lucan. 'Can anyone tell me how we got out of Death Row?'

'I jumped,' the Afghan declared brightly, 'I jumped through the gate. I can jump anywhere. Please can I go now and jump?'

'No,' said Lucan crossly, 'and that's not the answer to how we got out of the pen.'

'We got out because we worked together,' said the curly dog, McKlickety. 'That's the answer you wanted, isn't it, boss?'

'That's it,' Lucan agreed, 'and we've got to go on working together if we want to stay free. We've got to become a gang; that's how to survive, as a gang.'

'Great,' the Afghan could follow this idea, 'we'll be a gang and go round together chasing things.'

'Helping people,' the Labrador suggested.

'Generally having a good time,' the Clumber added.

'Go on,' Lucan said to the other two, 'how do you think we should carry on?'

'I'm vague,' the Boxer admitted, 'but I'm easy,' he added hurriedly. 'I'll go along with what the rest of you are doing. I'll just fit in.'

He hated to be noticed or made to decide things.

'I'm a country dog and I'm a loner,' McKlickety gave Lucan a cool look. 'But I'll work with a boss if he feeds me regular. Let's say I'll go along for the ride and quit if the going gets bumpy. Six dogs don't feed easy.'

'No one is going to come rushing to adopt any of us,' said the Clumber, 'we're all too big. People like puppies.'

'None of you knows what to do,' said Lucan. 'We want to be happy and we want to have fun and we want to stay together,' he reminded them carefully. 'So this is what must happen . . .'

At that moment Patrol Car 49 swung fast into Patrick Place.

'Got 'em!' said P.C. Malcolm Minster in triumph.

'We've seen them,' P.C. Lewis corrected him, 'but we have yet to get them!'

'Here boy! Here boy! Come here, boy!' P.C. Minster ordered, jumping out of the car. He made a grab for the Afghan, who let him get close because he hoped there might be something to eat.

'Follow me,' Lucan ordered, 'these are policemen and they shut dogs up. The old women must have set them on our trail.'

He leaped over a low garden wall and hurried out of sight around the corner of a gothic greenhouse choked with old vines. The other dogs dashed after him, even the Afghan found it very easy to sidestep away from P.C. Minster.

'If you played more rugby on Saturday afternoons, M.M, you'd tackle better,' P.C. Lewis called. He had not moved from his seat in the car.

Muttering crossly, P.C. Minster scrambled back behind the wheel and drove quickly into the next street hoping to cut the dogs off. They were just in time to see the old Labrador and the Clumber disappearing down another linking side street. With tyres screeching P.C. Minster drove in pursuit. In the next long street all the dogs were in sight cantering steadily at the pace of the slowest, but just as Patrol Car 49, grinding harshly in second gear, caught up with them Lucan ordered them all up a narrow connecting entry back into the street they had just left.

'These dogs have got a sense of what I'd call tactics,' P.C. Lewis was enjoying the chase very much. He particularly liked Sealyhams, but he was fond of all dogs.

When P.C. Minster drove whizzing round, back into Sutherland Street, there was not a dog in sight except a Jack Russell terrier on a lead with a very upright old gentleman.

'You look left uphill, I'll look right, downhill,' P.C. Minster ordered, 'they can't have gone far. I'll run alongside one, then you open your door and grab it!'

'Do I handcuff its front legs or its back ones?' P.C. Lewis asked, but got no answer. Very slowly, eyeing every front garden and side alley, P.C. Minster drove down the quiet, morning street.

In Hampden Terrace, the parallel street one block down the hill, Lucan and his gang were planning P.C. Minster's ruin.

'We have to deal with him firmly,' Lucan told the others. 'We need to use roads freely and we can't do that with a patrol car chasing at our heels. Now he thinks you're the easy catch,' he nodded at the Afghan hound. 'I want you to go up this small street, and show yourself in the big street when I tell you to, but only then.' Lucan talked slowly so that the Afghan could take it all in. 'You're very important because you're going to be the bait. Do you understand? Very important!'

The Afghan panted eagerly.

'Will there be more jumping?' he wanted to know.

'Later,' Lucan promised him, and the Afghan lolloped off cheerfully up the linking street to stand at the corner with Sutherland Street, just out of sight of the patrolling police car which was creeping along, spying up into every entry and pink-cherried front garden.

Lucan looked calculatingly along Hampden Terrace, and at the rest of the gang gathered there. A half-filled milk float was jingling softly towards them. The milk woman never stopped because she had two boys running full tilt all the time up and down front paths, picking up empty bottles and laying down full ones.

'Show yourself!' Lucan called to the Afghan. 'Give them a good look.'

The Afghan leaped out into the middle of Sutherland Street and barked.

'There's one,' P.C. Minster cried gleefully. 'It's the softy with long legs!'

Lucan heard the snarl of the patrol car's revving engine.

'Come back towards me a few jumps down the street, then stand still and look lost,' he ordered.

The police car came zooming up to the head of the side street.

'Now take it easy,' P.C. Lewis warned. 'If we creep up on him quietly I've got a chocolate biscuit here that I was keeping for my lunch. I'll hold it out through the door to him and grab him when he comes for it.'

'Good work, Lewis,' P.C. Minster breathed excitedly, 'these dogs are like vermin round here, messing the streets. Time we took a firm line!'

Patrol Car 49 coasted gently down towards the Afghan on free wheel. P.C. Lewis opened his door and leaned out with a snack biscuit.

'Food, boy, food!' he called encouragingly. 'Lovely sweety bicks!'

'Wait till they get up to you,' Lucan warned, as the Afghan sniffed appreciatively at the smell of warm chocolate.

'Now jump for your life towards me!' he ordered.

'Jump!' Lucan repeated with all his strength as the Afghan very nearly waited too long, tempted by the biscuit. 'Remember Victor!'

With a nervous sideways leap the Afghan spun away from P.C. Lewis's grasping hand and bounded headlong down towards Hampden Terrace. P.C. Minster crashed into second gear and drove full tilt after him. The Afghan was running on the left side of the car where P.C. Lewis still had the door open. P.C. Minster at the wheel was craning to see where the dog had got to. The one direction he was not looking as he drove out into Sutherland Street was to the right and that was where the milk float was purring along.

Patrol Car 49, travelling at about thirty miles an hour, ran smack into the milk float. This spun round on its axis, shedding half the racks of milk into the gutter, and ended up facing back the way it had come. The police car stopped dead in the middle of the street. P.C. Lewis just, and only just, hung on to his safety belt and missed falling out on his face. The chocolate biscuit in his left hand squashed to a muddy pulp.

'Oh no!' said P.C. Minster. 'Oh no!'

'Call yourself a policeman!' gritted the milk lady as a torrent of foaming cream swilled down the corner grid. 'When I've seen your Superintendent you'll be lucky if you get a job delivering coal!'

'Thus perish all our enemies,' said Lucan, licking a splash of yoghurt from his left forepaw. 'Now let's get down the hill and into Bristol while they're clearing this lot.'

Very impressed with the noise and the spectacle, the other dogs trotted obediently after him. Every now and then the Afghan took a well-deserved jump.

They came down the roof-steep slopes of Kingsdown, through the old houses and out into Newfoundland Road. Bristol was looking very lively: it was a sunny morning with the promise of showers to brighten it, the traffic was swirling down to the roundabout that leads on to the M32, and Lucan felt his spirits rising as he led the dogs at a scamper out on to the grass verge. There he could feel the surge and flow of traffic pelting in and out of the city.

'Now,' he said, 'before I was interrupted, we had agreed that we wanted to keep together and have fun.'

'After what you did to that police car,' said McKlickety, 'I think we can also agree that we all want to get a long way from Bristol.'

'Right,' Lucan nodded, 'and the way to do that and to have a great time is to use the motorways.'

The other dogs looked at him rather doubtfully.

'Not what I'd call a quiet life,' said the Clumber as three

Juggernaut lorries tailed each other round the roundabout.

'I've always been trained to be very wary of traffic,' the old Labrador hesitated. 'Look left, look right and then look left again, or is it the other way round?'

'The only way to have fun in this country now is to keep moving,' Lucan continued enthusiastically. 'You want a base, and I know just the place: near a motorway, easy on, easy off, get anywhere in a few hours. Get high up in a car or perched on the back of a lorry and the world's your oyster! Stick around with me and we can do all the things people really enjoy doing. We can drive fast, go to pop festivals, discos, football matches, the seaside, stately homes, car rallies, anything!'

'And when we get hungry do we chew rubber tyres?' McKlickety asked innocently.

'Motorway Service Stations have the best food in Britain,' Lucan told him severely 'and plenty of it, I've tried it and I've got the food all worked out.'

'What about warm fires and a comfortable rug?' asked the Clumber.

'Warm fires and a comfortable rug mean an owner,' Lucan explained, 'and we all know where owners got us to – Death Row.'

The other dogs stirred uneasily.

'Humans are great,' Lucan went on. 'I've nothing against them, they know how to have a good time, and we can't do without them. But they need to be handled and I know the way their minds work. Don't forget, I'm not like you, I can understand everything they say, not just pick out a word here and there like "to heel" or "walkies"! I'm not just a dog, I'm a super dog! You saw how I handled the old woman and you saw how I handled the police. How about trusting me and we all pull together. Right?'

'Right!' they all agreed, some more than others.

'So we're a gang,' Lucan continued, 'and a gang always has a name, and people get the most kicks out of a thing called Rock, so we're going to be the Rock Dog Gang and we'll all help each other to have a good time. Are you with me?'

'I'm with you, of course,' said the Boxer, talking very fast so that the words jumbled up together. 'I'll go along with the crowd. Very glad to. Great idea, this gang. Something I've always had at the back of my mind. But could you be a bit clearer about this Rock, what is it exactly? Not stones, I'm sure, or that round sweet stuff children eat to rot their teeth, but something else.'

'Rock is music,' Lucan explained. 'Rock is jumping about.'

'Jumping! Magic! Great! Magic!' said the Afghan.

'But much more than that,' Lucan went on. 'Rock is a way of looking at life. It's like the traffic here, it's how you get up and do things. Look, I'll show you what I mean. Follow me!'

A lorry swung past the dogs to join the short queue of traffic waiting to filter on to the M32 out of the city. Music was pouring from a cassette in the driver's cabin, and along the sides of the lorry was written 'Ippigen Bros. Ltd. Ropemakers Birmingham.'

'That's our direction: Birmingham,' Lucan called out happily, 'and that's our sort of lorry. Grabbing hold of it all and putting it together is what I call Rock. The tailgate's down; we've got about twenty seconds; if we all take a run down this grass slope we'll be up on the back of it before he gets away. Ready? Steady? Rock!'

The six dogs ran down the short hill, leaped up and landed, with varying thumps, on the empty back of the lorry.

4
First flight on the motorways

'Baby Baby' was playing on the stereo pack in the cabin. What with that and the traffic coming out of town and the gear shift of the engine, the driver never noticed the dog thumps from the rear. He edged out into the second lane and moved up the gears. Under a scatter of shower, rainbow and sunshine, the Rock Dog Gang sped out on to the motorways.

'This is the life!' Lucan told the others as they sat rather uneasily, watching Bristol rush away behind them. 'My owner had stereo in his car and he was always playing this when we went driving about. But that was before he got married.'

'Was he married for long?' the Labrador asked; she always liked family details.

'Only about three months,' Lucan answered thoughtfully, 'but it caused a lot of trouble. That's really why I'm here.'

'How sad! My owner was never married at all,' the Labrador told him. 'Of course she was blind. I used to guide her.'

'Why did she get rid of you?' McKlickety was rudely curious. 'Blind people don't usually get rid of guide dogs.'

'I kept leading her under branches,' the Labrador replied sadly, 'and she'd bump her head. I was very good with obstacles at my level, and first rate with crossing roads, but I never could remember to look up. I was really fond of her but in the end I had to leave.'

The other dogs were sympathetically silent for a moment.

'Are we going all the way to Birmingham?' the Clumber asked. 'I was wondering because she spilt all our breakfast down that hole this morning.'

'Only part of the way,' Lucan explained. 'We'll stop at a service station that I know well. Then there'll be plenty to eat.'

'Meat?' the Afghan suggested.

'Yes, meat is what we all need,' McKlickety agreed, and the others nodded.

'There'll be ham sandwiches,' Lucan said firmly. 'See! now we're filtering into a real motorway, a very fast one! This is the M4; it goes from London right into Wales, but we're not going there. We turn right at the Almondsbury Interchange where all the roads whizz over each other. It's the most modern crossroads in Europe. You'll enjoy that.'

'There's no hurry of course,' said the Boxer, 'I mean it's fine just sitting up here; but will we get to any of the things today that you mentioned: football matches, pop festivals and all that?'

'Not today!' Lucan replied crossly. 'You have to plan carefully to get to something like a football match. It's something you look forward to.'

'Have you ever got right in, actually to see a match?' McKlickety asked.

'Not quite,' Lucan explained. 'I was always left to look after the car.'

'I see,' said McKlickety.

'And now our gang has a name,' Lucan went on hurriedly to keep them from asking any more questions, 'it's time we all got our personal names straight. We'll need new ones now that we're starting a different way of living.'

'I'm going to go on being called McKlickety,' the curly black dog said firmly. 'It's a very unusual name for a dog. Really, it's the name of a mountain in Ireland and I like it.'

'I don't remember my name,' the Afghan said smugly. 'They were always calling something but I never used to answer. I want a really powerful, butch sort of a name, to go with what I've been doing today: wrecking police cars, terrorising old women and all that.'

'How about Khamsin?' Lucan suggested. 'That's the name of a hot desert wind in Egypt that sweeps everything before it at just this time of year.'

'And it's the name of a very hairy model of a Maserati car,' the Clumber added unexpectedly. 'I know because my owner drove one.'

'Twin cam heads, 320 horse power at 5500 revolutions per minute, a five speed gear box; quite a car to be called after,' Lucan put in.

'That sounds like a great name,' the Afghan commented seriously. 'I'll try to remember it. Khamsin. I like it!'

'Good,' said Lucan, turning to the Clumber, 'now I don't care what you used to be called, your new name has to be Squire.'

'Good enough,' the Clumber sounded pleased, 'and a lot better than the old one, I can tell you.'

'I had several names,' the Boxer put in. 'It all seemed to depend on who was talking to me.'

'Like what?' McKlickety asked.

'Oh, one was Gobby Joe and another one was Dumbo so perhaps a fresh start . . .'

' . . . is bound to be an improvement,' Lucan interrupted, because the Boxer had a nervous trick of just rattling on. 'We'll call you Cassius because he was a boxer of the other kind, very much admired. A great fighter and a very fine speaker.'

'Oh well,' the Boxer began, 'I'm not fussy and if you really think . . .'

'I'm sorry,' the old Labrador interrupted, nervously firm. 'I've had one name for a very long time now and I'm too old to change. Probably it's not the kind of name you're looking for but it will just have to serve.'

'What is it? It's probably a very good name,' Lucan asked encouragingly.

'Sheila,' the Labrador answered wearily, 'take it or leave it!'

Lucan was trying to think of something polite and truthful when their lorry swung off to the left and began to mount a curving hill.

'This is the Almondsbury Interchange,' he told the other dogs excitedly. 'See! we're leaving the M4 now and joining the M5 which will take us north to set up our base camp. The motorways get you everywhere in no time.'

'If we are going north,' said Cassius, 'then we are going to get very wet!'

It was quite true. Ahead of them were the low lines of the Cotswold Hills and piled above them was a dark shower cloud.

'Rain is not too bad if you've got good food in your stomach,' said Squire soulfully.

'Which we haven't,' added McKlickety meaningfully. 'Dogs don't get far without meat.'

Lucan knew he was having a problem of leadership. Something came to his mind that he had heard on T.V.

'They've got a thing called a Meat Mountain,' he said airily.

'Who has?' the others wanted to know.

'Europe has,' he told them. 'It's part of a thing called the Common Market.'

'I was always on a lead in a market,' Cassius put in, 'but they were full of things to eat.'

'The Common Market is bigger than anything else,' Lucan went on, racking his brain for things he had half listened to. 'It has lakes of butter and lakes of wine and a mountain of meat!'

'That sounds Rock,' said McKlickety. 'If you could get us to a Meat Mountain that would be really something.'

'I think they try to sell it cheaply to the Russians,' Lucan remembered.

'They'd do anything to keep it from dogs,' Cassius agreed gloomily.

'But we'll keep our eyes open,' Lucan encouraged them. 'If anything good is moving you'll find it on these motorways.'

As if to contradict him the rain blew in from the west on their very first stretch of the M5. For the first mile or two it rained a heavy April downpour. The wind of their passage blew ice cold through their fur and Lucan heard grumbles from behind.

'I'm not complaining, of course,' Cassius the Boxer began, 'I'm just wondering whether these conditions are usual when hitching, whether this rain . . .'

'Shut up,' Lucan ordered gruffly, 'or you'll never even sniff the Meat Mountain! A Rock Gang takes troubles and rides with them. We don't moan, we Rock, with rain, sun, snow, and if you don't Rock you drop off. Got it?'

Cassius looked nervously at the wet road streaming behind them.

'Oh quite, that's just how I feel,' he said hurriedly, and he kept quiet for several minutes.

Soon the clouds cracked open, first white, then gold, and in half a minute the sun, westering a little, was flooding everywhere, the sky was blue and the motorway steaming.

To keep their minds off food, Lucan set the dogs to spotting custom cars. Their first was an old Rover with a silver Viking's head on the bonnet, a row of brown oars painted down each side and a scarlet dragon's head painted on its boot.

'Here's another one coming up,' Khamsin called excitedly. 'It's got an even greater colour scheme and a light on top. I like it!'

'All sit quietly and don't look interested,' Lucan ordered. 'It's a police car, Khamsin. That's how they paint them, and the light on the top is to dazzle criminals!'

'Razor sharp!' said Khamsin. 'I guess I'm learning.'

The police Granada swept up behind the slow lorry and for a few moments the two policemen inside scowled at the six dogs lying behind the open tailgate. Lucan saw one speaking into his radio as if passing on information, then the car accelerated and shot past them.

'We are a bit obvious, aren't we?' McKlickety commented.

'We'll soon be getting off. I hope the police aren't waiting for us,' Lucan said. 'In future we must keep a much lower profile.'

'Like shut up and lie down,' the Afghan suggested.

'Yes, you're learning!' Lucan agreed.

Their motorway was twining smoothly between Gloucester and Cheltenham. Stumpy, sinister hills stuck up out of the plain. To one side Gloucester cathedral was white with sunshine against a great bank of purple rain cloud, to the other the big gasometer of Cheltenham was green against the long wave of the Cotswolds.

'This is where we get off,' said Lucan, standing up, 'at Strensham Services area. We're nearly at base camp.'

'What if the driver doesn't turn in?' McKlickety asked.

'We'll make him turn in,' Lucan replied confidently.

In fact their driver, Bert Cross of Handsworth, was looking forward to his tea in Birmingham and had no intention of stopping at Strensham Service Station. But he was just passing the first three stroke marker post for the turning into the Station when a long thump, like broken thunder, shook the thin metal wall at the back of his cab.

He took a quick glance over his shoulder through the rear window but could see nothing unusual. The dogs, who had hurled themselves in a pack at the cab wall, were now lying huddled up under the window out of sight.

'Staple my gizzard, that's the big end gone!' Bert exclaimed. 'And not another repair shop for thirty miles!'

Quickly, just before the turn off ended, Bert swung the lorry left into Strensham Service Station and drove very slowly towards the lorry parking area, straining his ears for more bad engine noises. He did hear one or two scraping, scrabbling noises, but he was never to know that this was the sound of the Rock Dog Gang leaving him as he slowed down to turn near the restaurant.

'I told you,' said Lucan proudly as he collected his

group together, 'just be firm and you're in charge of the whole motorway.'

'Now for the kitchens,' said Squire.

'Scrounging and scrumping,' panted McKlickety.

'Meat!' said Khamsin.

'Listen to me,' ordered Lucan sharply. Reluctantly the other dogs turned to listen.

'We mean to stay around here,' he went on. 'This is where we are each going to find a sponsor. So that means we want everyone here on our side. Right?'

'Right,' the Rock Gang agreed.

'That means there's to be no cocking up legs on walls or making messes. Only bored stupid dogs do that and humans never like it.'

'But boss!' Khamsin protested. 'It's our way of life!'

'It was our way of life,' Lucan corrected him. 'Intelligence is the ability to change. Don't argue.'

The dogs were respectfully silent.

'And another thing,' Lucan continued, 'no scrounging and scrumping. Humans don't like that either. We've got to live with people, not against them. In future the watchword is going to be "charm". No more snatch and grab. We're going to charm people into giving food to us and wanting us to come back for more. Charm is how you control people. No more owners; we just charm sponsors. That way we'll have an easy life and time for lots of fun.

'Any disagreements? Anyone want to beat up Strensham and district, bite the children, frighten the old ladies?'

'No boss,' Cassius said uneasily, 'but just what does this charm look like in action?'

'Just stand behind those bins and watch me, all of you. Then you'll find out,' Lucan told them.

He nosed about for a minute in a sack of waste and came

up with a big wicker fruit basket in his mouth. With this he walked over to the doors of the restaurant kitchen and waited. Soon, out came two cheerful giggly girls in white overalls. Promptly Lucan sat up on his haunches with the wicker basket in his mouth supported by his forepaws in a beseech position. He whimpered pitifully and wagged his bobtail.

'Oh bless him!' one of the girls laughed delightedly. 'Have you ever seen anything like that before, Lois?'

'Never, Sandra,' said the other. 'Isn't he lovely?'

'Keep him here half a mo, Lois,' said Sandra, and she wobbled back into the kitchen, clacking on her high cork heels.

Lucan needed no keeping, he was still propped up there a minute later when Sandra came out with a newspaper full of minced meat and cut off bits of fat. She put these carefully into Lucan's basket, almost filling it. Lucan put the basket down, reared up again and saluted with one paw to his forehead. Then he picked up the meat load again.

'Here, you lot,' Sandra called back into the kitchen, 'come and look at this.'

But before anyone could come out of the door Lucan was hidden away among the bins with the five other dogs. He dropped his basket casually in front of Khamsin the Afghan.

'Have some meat,' he said.

'That was magic!' Khamsin gasped.

'No it wasn't, it was charm,' Lucan corrected him. 'Most of us ended up in Death Row because we didn't use charm. A big dog costs money to feed. If they're going to spend money people want a bit of charm. So in future we give it to them. Look grateful, play tricks and you'll have a friend for life. Tomorrow, when you go out looking for

sponsors I want you to start working on it.'

'I think that was truly lovely,' Sheila said quietly. 'Tomorrow I'm going to work on it just as hard as I can.'

'Good,' said Lucan. 'Now let's eat this up and get moving for base camp.'

Every dog very carefully took his exact share of meat and for a while there were only munching chewing noises.

'Super!' said McKlickety, smacking his lips. 'If you can lay on meat like that you can lead me from here to China.'

'And talking of Super,' said Squire, 'how about Super as a new name for you? You deserve it after all the super things today!'

'All right,' Lucan agreed, 'but more as a title than a name. It's short for Superintendent, the police use it a lot. I'll be Super Lucan, Super for short. Now out into that lane and let's get to base camp before it gets completely dark.'

Alongside Strensham lorry park ran a little lane with two big *No Entry* signs on each side of the open gate between the lane and the service station. Just as the Rock Gang were making for this gate the high snarling sound of a small engine, driven hard, rose behind them. They turned to see a tiny low vehicle, topless and coloured khaki, zooming off the M5 and swerving through the petrol pumps straight towards them. As they scattered, it shot between the *No Entry* signs and swung right into the shadowy land with a squeal of smoking tyres. For a moment Lucan caught a glimpse of the driver, a young man with fair, windblown curly hair, laughing at the wheel and a girl in leather sitting next to him. They waved to someone in the direction of the kitchens. Then they were gone.

'Wow man!' Khamsin shook his floppy ears admiringly. 'Was that a hot rock custom car!'

5

A tower with a view

'That was a Mini Moke,' Lucan declared. 'They're quite rare now. They don't make them in this country any longer because drivers here are too soft. But they still make a few in Australia. All they are is a light chassis, an engine and a canvas top. In one of those you could really rock.'

'Drivers like that should be put in prison,' Sheila disapproved.

'You couldn't keep a real Moke driver in prison,' Lucan told her firmly, 'he'd break out! Come on, Gang, we're going in the same direction.'

Light was fading early as more rain clouds blew up from the west. Lucan led his gang through the *No Entry* gates, into the lane and over the bridge across the motorway. Quite sharply the sizzle and zoom of the speeding traffic fell away and they were in quiet reaches of Worcestershire with blackbirds defying each other from whitethorn bushes, and primroses clustered in deep ditches.

They padded purposefully through the village of Earls Priestly with brick cottages and yeoman farmsteads in black and white timbering lining the lane.

'There are two very pretty empty cottages on this crossroads,' Sheila observed. 'Perhaps we could settle in here. It would be handy for the shops and there would be sponsors for all of us.' Since she had got away from the lorry and the traffic noise she had been cheering up.

'Rock Dog Gangs do not live in pretty cottages,' Lucan told her firmly. 'And they try to keep miles away from shops. Once you live in a pretty cottage you're finished as a living, rocking dog. It's just a matter of time before they bury you at the bottom of the garden under some pretty flowers!'

Sheila did not look convinced.

'We go up here!' Lucan said, leaving the farm road and pushing up an overgrown path that climbed a wooded hill. It was almost night in the wood so all the dogs except Lucan were surprised when two dark towers loomed out high above the branches on the hilltop, like the gateway to a castle that had never been built.

'This is it,' said Lucan, 'Base Camp!'

'I'm sure it's very impressive,' Cassius said in his usual, roundabout way, 'I mean it's very tall and there's a lot of it. But, you won't mind my asking, can we live in it?'

'Live in it!' Lucan replied scornfully. 'We're not going to live anywhere. We're going to rock round all the motorways in Britain doing everything that people really rate. But you need a Base Camp and this is it. You can sleep in it and the rest of the world is for living in. Later, when we've finished with this country, we'll go rocking off to the Continent; everyone goes there, to Majorca mainly. But we'll always come back here to build up our resources. Come with me; you haven't seen the most exciting thing about Base Camp yet.'

He led them through the high broken arch between the

two towers. The trees ended and the sky was open to the sunset again, pale lemon and washed out green over the Malverns.

'There!' said Lucan. 'Even here we haven't lost it. We're still right on top of all the action.'

One steep field below them the M5 motorway cut ruthlessly through the countryside. On this side of the towers the noise hit them like a busy street, and the headlamps cutting north and south made the dying sun look dim and slow. Once, a few years ago, these towers had been in the very deepest depths of rural nowhere; now the cities had reached out with this bar of road, and quietness was suddenly fringed with gear changes and vibrant weights passing.

'Good,' said Lucan. He could see that the other dogs did not know how to react, it had been a long tiring day for them. Later they would see how convenient it all was; now they wanted to sleep. He took them into the left-hand tower up a bare, elegant 18th century staircase into the tower room. It smelt of pigeons, the floor was wooden and there were bales of straw around the walls and more straw on the floor. A cheap deal table and an old mattress showed that sometimes someone used the place, but tidily and rarely. It did not feel like a tramp's lair.

'Settle down, Gang,' Lucan told them. 'Pull more straw from the bales if you need it. Sleep close together and you won't feel the cold. I'll wake you in the morning and we'll plan everything out.'

Khamsin flopped asleep after only half a circle, he was a very young dog, almost a puppy. McKlickety and Squire pulled a bale into loose chunks and hanks. The others settled down in the straw and were soon asleep. Only Lucan, being a Super Dog, was not ready yet for bed. He

climbed the short wooden steps that led on upwards from the Tower Room, pushed the low swinging door open and stepped out on to the roof. He put his paws up on the battlements and looked around. It had been a good day, just about the best day he could remember. In many ways it was his first real day ever. He had begun to use the wits that had been idling before. Lorries he was not quite happy about. You got good views from them but they were rather too refreshing when it rained and he would have to work on the problem of using motor cars again.

From the wood below came the distinctive engine note of the dashingly driven Mini Moke. Perhaps the curly-haired driver lived in the next farm. The Moke sounded nearer, coming along the farm track; it was odd that he could see no headlights through the trees.

Lucan peered harder into the dusk. The Moke had not turned its lights on. That was cool perhaps, but very dangerous. He could just make out the dark shape as the little car moved bumpily over the fields. Lucan was sure there wasn't even a footpath there. The driver might be practising for a midnight motor rally. Dimly he saw it drive down a second field and disappear in a neat half circle of very young woodland on the edge of the motorway. There seemed to be earthworks and banks among the trees. The engine stopped.

Lucan waited for a long time, until night had settled on the country, but the Mini Moke's engine did not start again and he was determined to look further into the mystery the next day.

Down in the Tower Room the other dogs slept. The Afghan whined in an uneasy dream of jumping patrol cars. Lucan turned circle twice, out of habit, then settled down to sleep.

At just this very moment P.C. Malcolm Minster was raising a glass of elderflower sherry to toast Fran and Julie Bosker in their over-furnished back sitting-room.

'Your very good health, officer,' said Fran.

'Cheers, ladies!' P.C. Minster knocked his tiny glass back in one gulp and winced to find out how dry it was.

'Bottoms up!' said Miss Julie from the sofa where she was lying full length with her plaster cast leg on a side stool.

'And may I say success to our quest!' P.C. Minster added to hide the wry face he was making. 'The recapture forthwith of a particularly nasty set of animals.'

'Officer,' Fran Bosker shook her head to jingle her earrings, 'if you had seen them as I saw them this morning. Gnashing! Positively gnashing at me through the wire, you would not rest before you apprehended the pack of them. What worries me more than anything is the thought of what they may do to any kiddies unfortunate enough to cross them. Believe me, if it hadn't been for that wire . . .'

'Yes, Fran, old dear,' Miss Julie interrupted. 'You've

already told the officer that bit, and from his very unpleasant experience with them I'm sure he's as anxious to catch them as we are.'

'My presence here this evening, entirely unofficially and in off-duty hours, testifies to that,' P.C. Minster assured her. 'You ladies have been most helpful. The smallest clue as to a criminal's habits often leads to his downfall. If we look for that Bearded Collie, as you suggest, the others will not be far away.'

'And look out for cars, remember,' Miss Julie prompted him fiercely. 'His previous owner, a man of a very poor type if I may say so, assured me on the 'phone this evening that the dog was devoted, absolutely devoted, to travel in motor cars. Watch the roads! Watch the garages! That dog will hang about them.'

'It's the kiddies that worry me . . .' began Miss Fran.

'Damn you and damn the kiddies!' Miss Julie exploded. 'That dog has broken my ankle and damaged this officer's career prospects. Because of that dog's activities I am lying here on a bed of pain and this officer has been posted to a highly inconvenient new rota of duties. Where was it you said you had been posted, officer?'

'To motorway patrol on the M5 and the M4,' P.C. Minster smiled meaningfully.

'To the motorways! Ah!' Miss Julie smiled back, grasping the point.

'A very helpful appointment in view of our recent conversation,' P.C. Minster's smile grew even more sinister.

'Let's drink to the motorways!' Miss Julie reached for the bottle.

Grimly P.C. Minster watched the bitter liquid trickle into his glass.

6
Sponsors

Next morning it was raining and most of the dogs dozed fitfully or woke fretfully, so Lucan put them through what he called Battle Training. They had to jump along the crumbling arch that linked the two towers, dash down the ladders of the empty tower, out into the open, back into their Base Camp tower, up the staircases, on to the roof, over the arch and down again.

Sheila only did one circuit, but even Squire did five and Khamsin had to be stopped forcibly on his thirtieth round. By that time the sun was breaking through and Lucan sent them all out to scout for sponsors.

'Keep away from Strensham Service Area,' he said, 'that's my patch, and remember, don't eat breakfast until your sponsor is really keen to feed you. Make it so that you're doing them a favour, and never, ever, get too tied up with them. Rock Dogs don't have owners, not even friends, they just have the Gang! See you all here this evening and we'll work out the next fun routine.'

So off they went, through the wood, down the track and out to the villages. When Lucan was alone he trotted off across the fields down to the little wood of new trees by the motorway. He climbed a steep bank, shouldering his way through little conifers, elderbushes and trailing brambles, then found himself sliding on all four legs to land bump on hard tarmac. All around him in the clearing were heaps of gravel, barrels of tar, old boilers, grit piles, salt heaps and battered plastic road markers. Weeds were growing everywhere and it had been years since any of the heaps had been cut into. Between the overhanging bushes a narrow road led off and he followed it, padding over leaf mould. Two turns and he was out standing just above the noise and stir of the M5. Across the little road was an unpainted sign reading:

Motorway Repair Services
No Entry
Strictly Private

The sign could be pushed aside, because there were scrape marks on the gravel, but no workmen had been here for ages.

Lucan walked back into the secret clearing. Once again the air was very still, even the birds seemed to have given the place up. But facing him was a big brick garage with glass brick windows and rusty metal doors. The Mini Moke must live there. Lucan jumped up on to a barrel and tried to peer through the glass brick windows but he could only see dark twisted shapes.

Perhaps there was a crack in the doors. He leapt down and snuffled at the side with the hinges. There was an old sort of smell. He sniffed again: metal, china, fabric, but definitely old. Not at all Rock.

'Hello there! What brought you here?'

The voice was so unexpected that Lucan sprang round and barked once, quite fiercely, at the speaker, then wished he hadn't.

It was the fair-haired young man, dressed now for farm-work in jeans, wellington boots and a denim shirt with sleeves rolled up. His arms were roughly tattooed with hearts and games of noughts and crosses. On one arm was written *Lena* and on the other *Sandra*. He had a strong West Country accent.

'What are you doing nosing round my shed, eh?' the young man sounded quite friendly, he was smiling, but also he was looking warily about the clearing. He crossed it and went a few steps down the little link road to see if anyone was there, then came back satisfied.

By this time Lucan had worked out a new approach. As the young man came across to him, Lucan wagged his bob-tail, rolled over foolishly on his back and wiggled his legs in the air, yawning as he did so. This worked. The young man laughed, bent over and started to tickle Lucan's chest, talking all the while in the stupid way people do talk to dogs when there are no other humans around.

'What is it, then? What is it? You want your tummy tickled, do you? Well, you shall have it! What brought you here, eh? eh? eh? You come nosing around Ben's secret store, did you? Well, it's a good job you didn't bring anyone else nosing around with you! Bite me, would you?'

Lucan had given him a playful nip to encourage the flow of interesting nonsense.

'I'll give it you! I'll give it you! You want to buy grotty old antiques, do you? Well, boy, you can't have them. They've all been nicked anyways in there. And they don't belong to Ben, but they sort of belong to Jerry Joiner. Ben's just looking after them, like he's going to look after you. Just you come along with me, boy, and don't you be bringing any of your mates back here with you. You're not one of the rozzers' dogs, are you? No, you're too good-looking. Not the type.'

All this time Ben was checking on Lucan's collar, which gave only his name away.

'Lucan, eh? Come on, Lucan, then!'

Lucan leaped alertly to his feet, barked, and gave Ben a 'ready-for-anything' look. The bark was a mistake. Ben looked round nervously.

'Shhhh! Quiet, boy, quiet! Come along o'me.'

Lucan followed close at his heels as the young man turned up a narrow gully leading through the earthworks to the fields. Just next to the hedge was a big red tractor with a covered cab. Here Ben looked doubtfully at Lucan so Lucan helpfully leaped up into the cab, leaving plenty of room for Ben on the driver's seat.

'Ain't you the matey one!' Ben laughed again and looked pleased. He swung up into the seat, gave Lucan more hugs and silly talk, then started the engine. The tractor set off through fields along the side of the motorway, heading, as Lucan had guessed, in the direction of

Strensham Services Area, where they had got off the night before.

Lucan felt pleased but puzzled. It was a good job, he thought, for the young man's sake, that he wasn't a police dog because if he had been he could have collected a full criminal dossier on him in no time. He seemed a pleasant young man, fond of dogs; yet stolen property was bad news and apparently he had a whole hut load of it. But it 'sort of belonged' to Jerry Joiner, whoever he was. Lucan decided that he would stay around and find out. Though he had no very kind feelings about the Police, Lucan was on their side every time when it came to stolen property. Wayne used to watch all the cops and robbers serials on the telly and Lucan had watched them with him, so he knew what happened to criminals who hid nicked antiques. Ben must be saved, even if it meant trundling round muddy fields in slow tractors.

They drove in to the service area.

'I think you ought to hang about a bit,' Ben told Lucan, so Lucan barked cheerfully to show how stupid he was and followed Ben to the back of the restaurants.

'Well, look what the wind's blown up,' a young waitress came out covered in smiles. Lucan recognised her as the girl who had been riding in the Mini Moke, dressed in leather. Just behind her was the girl who had filled his basket with meat. This time she had a tray of coffee cups. When she saw Lucan her face lit up.

'It's my very own wonder dog,' she cried, 'that's him, the one I told you about with the lovely manners. Where did you pick him up, Ben?'

'Oh, back on the farm,' said Ben vaguely, so Lucan guessed that the girls were not in the secret of the hidden garage. 'You've met him before, have you, Sandra?'

'Oh, 'e's lovely, 'e is,' Sandra bent down and gave

Lucan kisses. She had very little make-up on except around her eyes, which were blue and green shadowed, so he gave her a careful lick. All three sat down on a step to drink their coffee and Lucan settled to listen to them. The girl who had been in the back of the Mini Moke was called Lena, which explained the two names tattooed on Ben's arms.

'Well,' said Lena, 'tonight's the great gig, isn't it? Are we really going through with it all punk like we decided?'

'Yeah!' said Ben cheerfully. 'It's make or break for us tonight. No more soft rock!'

Lucan listened intently; he seemed to have dropped by accident into exactly the scene he was looking for, though a little old fashioned as you might expect out here in the sticks.

'The Road House Wreckers,' Sandra sniffed. 'What a name for a group! How do you think we'll go down?'

'Fighting!' Ben declared. 'Just keep socking the words and the music out at them. If they shout or throw glasses, throw the glasses back at them but don't stop singing. That way you can't lose!'

They were all very nervous, though Ben and Lena were pretending to be ice cool. Lucan learned that Ben was lead guitar and there were three others in the group called Billy, Nick and Toad. They had not made any mark playing straight Pop so tonight they were hoping to break through as Punk Rockers at a gig in Tewkesbury at a place called 'The Floury Miller'.

Lucan felt like hugging himself. He had never been quite sure how to fit into discos and pop concerts as a dog, but now he could see himself sitting on the stage at the centre of it. Should he take the rest of the Gang, he wondered? Probably no; they would be tired, and six dogs might be harder to fit in among the electronics. Meanwhile, this lot had got to start loving him.

While they were finishing their coffee and Lena was trying out the words of 'Don't kill me for dreaming', Lucan slipped around the corner to some tubs of flowers which he had seen outside the restaurant. He picked two red tulips and came back with them carried carefully in the lower part of his mouth so that he didn't slobber on them. When they saw him the two girls squealed delightedly.

'Romeo! Romeo!' and

'Who's the lucky girl?'

Lucan laid one at Sandra's feet and the other one, just a little bit wet, at Lena's. Then he sat back on his haunches and did a little bob with his head.

'Strewth,' said Ben. 'If I hadn't seen it I wouldn't have believed it!'

'Isn't he a poppet!' said Lena.

'You could teach a dog like that tricks,' Ben went on.

'Tricks!' Sandra exclaimed. 'He could teach you tricks. Teach you a thing or two with the girls, he could. Couldn't you, my love?'

The girls screamed with laughter, Ben looked just a little put out and Lucan got more hugs and kisses. That just about clinched the deal, he thought, they'd take him along to their gig for sure after that.

Coffee time was over, he heard them arranging to meet on the green at Earls Priestly to be picked up by the others in a van at seven o'clock, then he and Ben went back to the tractor.

'Coming along for the ride, are you, lad?' Ben asked. 'I'll have to watch you or you'll be taking over and driving!'

Roaring with laughter Ben got up beside Lucan in the cab.

'Very funny,' Lucan thought, 'give me push buttons

instead of a gear lever and I'd drive you off the road any day!'

He decided to stay with Ben until teatime to find out all about him. But when Ben went to the farm where he worked, Lucan decided to keep out of the yard partly because it was very mucky with eighty Friesian cows, and partly because there were two very ill-natured Welsh black and white sheepdogs running on a long chain. Lucan knew that dogs on running chains developed sly ugly natures, and Welsh Sheepdogs were extra cunning creatures even at their best. So he waited out in the fields and followed Ben whenever he went out in the tractor or to call the cows. Ben shared his lunchtime sandwiches, which were ham with mustard, and tomato with yeast spread. There would be time later to get Ben off the mustard and yeast.

After milking, Ben drove home on a battered old Triumph motor bike. Lucan was sad that he wasn't offered a lift, but he galloped along full tilt behind to find that Ben lived in one of the village council houses. The front garden was full of potato rows and Ben's father, who dug the garden, did not like dogs, so Lucan went back to Base Camp.

Up in the tower room four of the dogs were waiting for him but Sheila was not there.

'I met her in Strensham,' Squire reported. 'She asked me to tell you that she wasn't quitting the Gang but she'd found a very nice old lady sponsor who liked to lean on her when she went down the garden and it might be late before she got back.'

'Hmm!' Lucan nodded. 'That dog needs to be needed. I don't reckon we'll see much more of her. How did the rest of you get on?'

'I struck lucky,' McKlickety reported. 'Met a

gamekeeper, works for the National Trust on a stately home. He's quite educated, and glad of help, excellent fellow!'

'Good,' said Lucan. 'How about Squire?'

'Landed right on my feet,' Squire said smugly. 'I came across this businessman, in a small way mind you, he's a grocer, well, self-service to be exact. People like him always welcome a dog on the premises to watch what the kiddies get up to at the freezer.'

'Feed well?' Lucan asked.

'Oh moderato, you know, the golden mean, don't want to put on weight; but three square meals a day at the usual times. Can't complain.'

'Ten circuits tomorrow morning,' Lucan ordered. 'Rock dogs never get fat.'

'I don't want to complain, you realise,' Cassius said. 'But this isn't the area where my class of people tend to live. I'm a quite unashamed suburb lover and out here in the country you rarely . . .'

'Did you find a sponsor?' Lucan interrupted.

'Well, actually, in a word, no,' the Boxer replied so sadly that even McKlickety made no sharp comments. Lucan sighed and made a mental note to look out for a retired couple with plenty of time on their hands.

'I got a sponsor and he's great!' the Afghan declared proudly.

'What does he do?' Lucan asked.

'Nuffin'!' replied Khamsin. 'But he throws sticks for me and he never gets tired.'

'Well, you've hit the bull's eye,' Lucan complimented him and went on quickly. 'Now I don't know about the rest of you but I feel like a brisk training run before I turn in, so I'll say "Good night" now. Tomorrow when we're all here we'll get down to real planning.'

Rather surprisingly only Cassius offered to run with him. The other dogs all avoided his eye and flopped down on the straw as if they were tired out.

'Sorry, Cassius,' Lucan said hastily. 'But it's going to be an S.A.S. type run this evening. Real rough stuff, I don't think you'll keep up with me!'

And with that he was out on the staircase and on his way to the village green to meet Ben and the girls.

7
Punk punch-up

It was a still, dull evening, growing dark early; the traffic sounds on the motorway carried clearly over the fields in the windless air. A night for music, Lucan thought, and, who knows, perhaps a bit of aggro on the side! It was a pity he hadn't been able to bring the others, but that could come later. After all, they were only truly interested in eating; fun was an acquired taste.

Ben and the two girls, all wearing long macs, were waiting in the bus shelter on the green.

'Look who's here!' Lena called as he peered into the shelter.

'Our lucky mascot. Now we're all right!' Sandra seemed pleased.

Lucan blinked and looked again. The view in the dark shelter was very odd. Both girls were wearing fluorescent lipstick and all three of them had day-glo spray on their hair.

'We're ghouls, Lucan!' Ben boomed in a spooky voice. 'You've got in with a bad lot!'

'No need to tell me that,' Lucan thought. What did puzzle him, however, was who was Ben's real girl friend, Lena or Sandra?

'Meet Lucan!' Ben went on. 'He's a dog, but he's got nine 'O' Levels and he works as a disc jockey on BBC One!'

Then Lucan noticed that there was a fourth person in the shadows of the shelter, a ten-year-old boy, very like Ben in the face but thinner and more serious.

'Meet my brother Kevin, Lucan. Kevin, meet my mate, Lucan,' Ben finished.

Deciding that this was the right time to impress, Lucan went up to Kevin and offered his right forepaw. Kevin solemnly shook it.

'What did we tell you?' the girls chorused. 'Isn't he more human than us?'

'Uncanny, innit?' said Ben.

Ben and the two girls started to tease each other about their day-glo make-up, but Kevin just stared intently at Lucan, watching everything he did. This bothered Lucan and he wished that he had not shaken hands like that. He looked away so as not to appear to be listening to Ben and the girls, but when he looked back Kevin was still gazing at him with just a hint of a grin on his pale, high cheekboned face. Finally, Kevin gave Lucan a long firm wink. Lucan tried desperately to look stupid, even pretending to hear a mouse in one corner of the bus shelter.

The arrival of the van from the direction of Kings Priestly saved Lucan from any more tricks. It hooted loudly as it drove up. Two young men were sitting on the front seat next to the driver: a solid, bearded man of about thirty.

'We've got a mascot,' Lena called out.

A chorus of groans came from the van as Ben opened the rear doors.

'Not another one!'

Inside, the van was three-quarters full of percussion, guitars, amplifiers, a wardrobe and reels of flex. Seated amidst it all were Squire, McKlickety and Khamsin. Lucan and his party scrambled in.

'Hi Gang!' said Lucan. 'So we all made it except for Cassius.'

It was fortunate that dogs are quite unable to blush.

As they drove on to the motorway the dark night turned to a shifting white wall in their headlights and a warning light was flashing to tell all vehicles to reduce speed to 30 m.p.h.

'It'll be worse at Tewkesbury,' Ben warned, 'fog always clings close to the river.'

'P'raps not many'll turn up,' said Nick in the front, gloomily.

'Ah well! There'll be fewer to throw things at us,' Lena giggled nervously.

It took a quarter of an hour to make the three miles to the Tewkesbury Gate 9 off the motorway, the fog was so thick. By that time Lucan had worked out that Bill was Squire's grocer sponsor and played bass guitar. Nick was McKlickety's gamekeeper from the National Trust and he played saxophone. The fat bearded driver was called

Toad, he was the manager and played the drums, he was also Khamsin's sponsor, the one who threw sticks all day. Kevin, Ben's little brother, was the groupie who handled the electronics.

'The Floury Miller', where the gig was being held, was the basement of an enormous brick mill by a dark back-water of the Severn. They crept there by mist-shrouded side streets and parked cautiously on the edge of the river bank. Even out here by the thin reeds and gloomy water the noise from 'The Floury Miller' was deafening. A group was playing, amplified up to the topmost.

'They'll be so deaf after this lot that they won't hear us,' Nick muttered.

The dogs kept out of the way as the van was unloaded, then followed the Road House Wreckers and their gear in by a back way. Now the whole solid mill basement was shaking to 'Don't Care, Don't Cry, Don't Sleep All Night'. It was being played by the first of the two groups featured that evening, a semi-pro local bunch from Evesham called 'The River Boys'.

'They got their bass all screwed up as usual,' Bill shouted.

'T'aint their bass's fault. It's their mikes. Cheap equipment,' Toad bellowed back. 'Not like ours! We'll show 'em!'

'Sure, Toad! We'll show 'em!' Ben agreed.

As the group got out of their long macs and finished making up, Lucan was impressed at what a lot they had to show. Everyone wore tight black plastic trousers. The girls had long pink jumpers and, of course, their hair and lips were luminous. They carried black guitars, but these were not wired up, so whatever they did to them would not be heard. Lucan decided they were there for visuals and they certainly looked punk with their heavily blackened eyebrows. The men wore collarless grey shirts and black waistcoats except for Ben who, being lead guitar and vocalist, just wore a waistcoat and had a long, artificial wound with seventeen stitches in it painted across his throat. His hair was dyed orange, but he had such a pleasant natural face that the effect was not convincingly nasty.

'What do you think?' McKlickety asked.

'Very amateur,' Lucan replied, 'but we've got to support them if there's trouble.'

'And there will be!' Squire prophesied, his eyes drooping mournfully.

'May I bite if there's aggro?' Khamsin asked eagerly.

'Only nips in the fleshy part of the leg,' Lucan told him, 'and only if they're looking the other way. We don't want to run into anything head on.'

The music next door stopped in the middle of a drum roll.

'Someone's got at them and pulled the plugs out,' Ben declared. 'See you keep a close eye on ours, Kev! Anyone comes near, tell Toad, he'll plug 'em.'

'Yeah, you tell me. I'll plug 'em,' Toad growled. Lucan could see why he got on well with Khamsin.

Next door a very mixed noise of cheering and booing ended the brief silence. A door was flung open.

'You're next,' a voice called, 'and watch out! We've got a rough crowd here tonight.'

'Hold my hand, Ben, I'm frightened,' said Sandra.

'And mine, Ben, I'm scared stiff,' said Lena.

Ben went on holding both their hands, so Lucan still didn't know which one was his real girl friend. They filed on to the stage which was lit with a mix of white and green lights. Ben was holding the girls, the rest of the group were heaving in the percussion and electronics.

Immediately there was a threatening roar of sound from the darkness where the audience stood. Khamsin growled.

'Just anyone step out of line,' he threatened.

The dogs all peered anxiously through gaps in the partition and holes where people had thrown missiles through the walls. Toad was very slowly kitting up his drums with little Kevin helping him.

'And now, folks,' the resident Deejay called into his microphone, 'if you didn't like the last lot you're sure going to like our next group. This is the top of the evening, the Road House Wreckers, and believe me they're really a wild lot!'

'Wild lot, my eye!' a voice called out. 'Them two girls work at the Service station and that's Ben Short from Earls Priestly!'

'What's he short of?' another wit cried out.

'I ain't short on hard fists,' Ben roared back, in a heavy American accent mixed with a West Country drawl, 'as I'll show any o' you that comes up here!'

This brought a cheer, Ben rode the tide, pulled an empty bottle of beer from the waistband of his black plastic trousers, pretended to drink from it and threw it casually over his shoulder. Unluckily it fell plump into the middle of Toad's snare drum, splitting the skin.

'Hey, you've bust me flippin' drum!' Toad complained.

This brought a roar of laughter; Ben gave a signal to the group.

'Hear this, boys and gals!' he called. 'We're gonna give you a real gritty version of an old Elvis classic, 'Ain't nuthin' but a Hound Dog,' and we sure hope ya like it.'

Rather raggedly the group began. There were murmurs and catcalls from the darkness of the crowd.

'They're not pushing the beat,' Lucan complained.

'How can they when one of the drums is bust?' Khamsin defended Toad.

Lucan could tell it was going to be a flop. There was just not enough noise, the words were coming over too clearly and though Ben was throwing himself about the stage the girls were hardly wriggling their hips. A glass came lobbing over, then bounced on the woodwork.

'If we don't do something, they've had it!' Lucan told the others.

'Who shall I bite?' Khamsin wanted to know.

'Can any of you pick out rhythm?' Lucan asked.

'Is he the one who threw the glass?' Khamsin demanded. The rest were not too sure.

'Call yourself a Rock Gang and you can't groove to rhythm,' Lucan snarled. 'Look, just follow me, step exactly when I step and keep grinning at the audience whatever they throw.'

He pushed the stage door open. Stepping stiff-legged and moving his shoulders exactly to the beat, he began a curve across the stage in front of Toad but behind the rest of the group. The other dogs followed him, nose to tail, stepping when he stepped, first McKlickety, then Squire, and Khamsin last. Only Toad realised why the groans turned to a delighted roar of cheering and a rhythmic clap from some of the fans, but Ben pitched furiously into the words and the song ended with loud applause and mock barking just as Khamsin, the last of the dogs, filed off the stage.

'Well, that's given them a start,' said Lucan, 'but we can't do that again. They're on their own now.'

'Can't I go back on?' Khamsin was panting eagerly, 'I don't mind being cheered!'

'Give the fans a breather,' McKlickety advised, 'they're overcome by your visuals.'

But the fans were not giving the Road House Wreckers much of a breather. Ben announced the next number, 'Someone's gonna get their shins knocked in tomorrow,' twisted his face up into a bitter pout and tore his waistcoat off to show a whole set of dreadful wounds and bruises, all put on with greasepaint. A storm of wolf whistles almost drowned his opening words, two more glasses and a bottle came looping out of the dark from the left hand corner of the hall.

Ben, Lena and Sandra were all clinging tightly together over Ben's mike.

'Look out, Baby,' they sang, squinnying out at the crowd.

'It must be you
Causes the pain
That I'm goin' through.
Yeah, yeah, yeah, yeah, yeah!'

'Well, why don't you all shut up then?' a voice called out.

'Move fast!' Lucan ordered. 'Round the side. It's that group standing near the bar. We've got to create a diversion.'

'Great!' said Khamsin. 'Aggro at last!'

'Don't bite anybody hard,' Lucan urged, 'anyone that pretends that this is really hard punk deserves to have a few rocks thrown at him.'

The Afghan was so keen that the other dogs were not needed. Khamsin came bouncing down an aisle, took three sharp nips at the calves of a bunch of Tewkesbury rockers gathered at the bar, and then went darting out through a side door almost before they'd begun to howl. When they came chasing out after him, Khamsin had disappeared and the other dogs were standing in the foyer confusing things.

'Give 'em hard looks,' said Lucan and all three tried, but only McKlickety managed to look very fierce because Clumbers never look anything but dignified and Bearded Collies just look absentmindedly cuddly. Still, it gave the group a chance to get back in control and the disco owner had time to 'phone for the police. Lucan led the other dogs backstage again out of trouble.

The next number, 'Corridors of Power,' was not true Punk Rock so it came over better.

'Your Bill's handing them a cool hard bass,' Lucan told Squirc.

'He took six aspirins before he started out,' Squire explained. 'So he's probably only just getting the top of his head back on.'

'And Ben can really sing when he's not trying to gargle with gravel,' McKlickety said.

Soon half the hall was dancing, some even doing the Hustler in a long line with their arms waving while the rest were doing the usual pogo-stick.

'Look, they're jumping!' said Khamsin. 'Will it be all right if I join in?'

'No, it won't,' Lucan was firm. 'They're quiet now in their own way, so leave them.'

Disaster came with the next item.

Lena took Ben's microphone and smiled nervously.

'Now, folks,' she announced. 'I'm going to sing one of our own little numbers that we're hoping to cut into a disc sometime before the noo year . . .'

'If I were you,' said a voice, 'I'd bury it in one of Ben's manure heaps!'

'It's called "Treacle and Jam",' Lena went on.

'And which one are you?' the voice demanded.

'Give the girl a chance,' Ben shouted back, 'or I'll plug you one!'

'You and Mrs Riley!' yelled another voice.

Ben gave the sign and the group thundered into action. This time Ben was the visuals. He was still stripped to the waist and now he scowled and struck a pose that flexed his muscles, the lights went red and Lena clung to him as she sang:

'I don't care for treacle,
I don't care for jam,
But what I like
On a fast motor bike
Is a real hard hunk of man!'

'Oh dear!' said Lucan.

'Get 'em,' roared the fans, and a wave of them came scrambling up on to the platform. Ben seized the microphone stand and pushed one invader back with its tripod feet. Bill swung a stool, Nick sat wishing he were back watching birds for the National Trust. Toad sank his head in his hands. It was the dogs who saved five hundred pounds' worth of second-hand equipment. They charged on to the stage snarling ferociously and baring their teeth in real punk style. If only Ben could have looked like that, Lucan thought. The fans on the platform backed off hurriedly. Then there was a sharp whistle blast from the foyer, various shouts of 'Coppers!' 'Rozzers!' 'Pigs!' and 'Police!' and a general wild scrummage began.

Back against the lighted foyer door Lucan saw at least three men in flat uniform caps. For a horrid second he recognised P.C. Minster and P.C. Minster recognised him, then someone finally got to the plug and all the lights went out.

Lucan got the other dogs outside within seconds. The fog was swirling even thicker. They had come out a back way on to the towpath, divided from the main crowd of fans by a narrow, weed grown mill race. Lucan spotted P.C. Minster furiously elbowing young people out of his way as he hurried to get on to the dogs' trail. Lucan took a chance, jumped into clear view and barked loudly. P.C. Minster swung round, recognised him, dived forward and fell headlong into two feet of mud and burr grass in the old mill race.

'Now let's lie low in the van and hope Toad hustles a bit this time,' Lucan ordered. But, just in case, he hid Squire and McKlickety in the wardrobe, Khamsin under some loose sacks, and himself under the driver's bench seat. This was fortunate because Ben had an argument trying to collect their fee from the manager, and when the van finally got moving the police had put a barricade across Leet Street. P.C. Minster was not manning it because he had been sent off by the Police Sergeant to change and get dry, but it was obvious what the police were looking for.

'We believe you have a troupe of performing dogs as part of your act,' the policeman at the barrer said, leaning through the open window and shining his torch into the back of the van.

'Entirely unrehearsed, officer,' Ben replied truthfully, 'and nothing to do with us. We'd like to lay hands on them ourselves. They wrecked our gig!'

'Bit of trouble, eh! Smashed any equipment?' the policeman asked hopefully.

'No, we saved that,' Ben replied. 'Toad here sat on it.'

'Well, keep an eye open for these dogs. They're supposed to be a dangerous set of animals that have escaped from a good home in Bristol. I don't mind telling you that one of our blokes, who fell into the river back there, is doin' 'is nut about them. I always say that once a constable has let a crime get on 'is mind, obsessed with it, like, he's passed his usefulness and needs to be directed kindly to something else. Still, it takes all sorts to make a force. I'll give you good night.'

'Good night, officer,' the group chorused.

'And watch out for the fog,' the talkative policeman raised the barrier and the van nosed carefully through the streets.

'Did you hear that?' asked Lena.

'A dangerous set of animals! Our mascots!' Sandra exclaimed.

'Load of old cobblers,' declared Ben scornfully, 'there's been a mix up. Wonder where they are, though? Think we ought to hang about and wait for them?'

'What, in this fog?' said Toad. 'Not likely!'

Sandra screamed shrilly as Lucan put his paw on her foot.

'Come on out, gang,' he called, and the other dogs emerged from sacks and wardrobes to cries of 'Sock me!' ''ere!' 'Christmas!' and more hugs and kisses. As Lena said,

'You could almost believe they were human!'

Ben spoke for all of them when he declared that if they had escaped from a home in Bristol it must have been for a very good reason.

But it was not a cheerful group that headed back up the motorway.

'No one will ever ask us to a gig again,' said Bill sadly, 'not this side of the Severn, anyway.'

'Well, if that's how you feel, Kevin and me have still got motocross to fall back on, haven't we, Kev?' Ben asked breezily. 'P'raps that's going to be our road to fame.'

'Where's the next round, Ben?' Bill asked.

'Dymock Common, next Monday,' Ben replied.

'What are you riding now?' Nick asked.

'A Kawasaki, a KX 125, lovely job! 27 b.h.p. at 10,000 revs. Brrrrm! Brrrrm! That was Ben that was!'

'I hear Kev's riding now,' Nick went on. 'That true, Kev?'

'Yeah,' said Kev shyly.

'How old are you, Kev?'

'Ten!'

'Strewth! On the race track already!'

'Kev's in the intermediate schoolboy class,' Ben explained, 'rides a Yamaha, nippy bike, good as mine on corners.'

'How do you afford all this, Ben, on what old Higman pays you?' Toad looked cunning, Ben's face went blank.

'Oh, we don't pay it!' Kevin laughed. 'We've got a sponsor, that's Jerry. Ben reckons it costs Jerry three thousand nicker a year clear to keep us two in motocross.'

'Lovely job!' said Bill. 'Glad some people can afford it. Who's Jerry, Ben?' He looked curiously across at Ben, who was not looking at all pleased. Lucan was listening hard.

'Jerry Joiner,' Ben replied shortly, 'bloke I know, lives in Elmberrow Hall at the back of Bredon Hill. Doesn't ride himself but he's keen.'

'Oh aye,' said Bill.

There was no more talking in the van after that until it pulled up in Earls Priestly where the dogs disappeared into the fog. Lucan was anxious that no one should have any idea of the direction of Base Camp.

Back in the Tower Room, poor Cassius had spent a lonely evening as Sheila had still not got back from her new sponsor. So they told him all the exciting things he had missed at Tewkesbury.

'It was a real rave up,' Khamsin boasted. 'I must have bitten fifty people and there was jumping going on all the time! At these discos everybody jumps. I'm going to go regularly.'

'If you bite fifty people every time you go you'll empty all the discos in Worcestershire,' McKlickety pretended to look worried.

'I wish I could get a sponsor and have fun like the rest of you,' said Cassius sadly. 'The trouble with me is that I've got this punched-up face.'

'And that trick of slobbering,' McKlickety added meanly.

'And this trick of slobbering,' Cassius agreed gloomily, 'which is, however, be it said, considered a good mark by many judges at high-class shows. I suppose they don't have dog shows in Worcestershire often, do they?'

'Rock Gangs despise them,' Lucan told him. 'Dog shows are just humans using dogs for their looks and not valuing them for what they really are! It's exploitation. If women can get Equal Rights then so can dogs. That's why I'm against dog shows, but I promise you, Cassius, we'll get you a really super sponsor within the next week!'

'Though I'm not sure,' he went on thoughtfully to himself, thinking of Jerry Joiner and motocross, 'I'm not sure that sponsors are always safe people to have around. Maybe next Monday at Dymock Common I'll find out!'

8

Marathon Sunday

Next morning, which was a Sunday, Sheila woke them all very early.

'Hello!' she called cheerfully. 'I'm back!'

'Hello!' a sleepy chorus drifted from the bales of straw.

'Bet you thought I'd gone for good,' she said.

'No, but we were worried about you,' Lucan replied, rather untruthfully.

'Has something gone wrong with your domestic arrangements?' Squire asked.

'Oh no! I've got a lovely comfy warm box, padded too, at the foot of my old lady's bed. Snug as a bug, I am. My old lady's very religious, which is nice, but it means she spends most of her Sundays at Church, helping with parish breakfasts and the Deaconess's Welcome Tea, and of course that's no place for a dog. So I've popped back to see if I can do anything for you.'

'We're going on a Sunday outing,' Lucan told her.

'That sounds very nice,' said Sheila. 'I'll come along. They say travel broadens the mind.'

'This is going to be Marathon Sunday,' Lucan announced, jumping up on a bale to make it sound important. 'Today the Rock Dog Gang are really going to

hit the motorways. We're going to Circumnavigate the Midlands!'

'Great!' said Khamsin, leaping up, ready for off.

'Will we be back in time for a meal?' Squire wondered.

'Will we ever get back?' Lucan challenged them. 'This is an adventure! This is risk! This is what we escaped for! Wheels rolling, the wind streaming through our fur, everything depending on our judgement of a driver's intentions.'

'Where do we go? Not that I'm worried, but curious, you know,' Cassius assured the others.

'Come up on the roof and I'll show you,' Lucan ordered, and they all climbed up to gaze out over the battlements. The mist had gone, there was a little sun, but clouds were streaming over fast from the west.

'We go north that way,' he pointed, 'up to Birmingham, which is very fine with huge buildings everywhere.

Then we leave this M5 to cut along the M6 to join the M1. That's the tricky bit. Then we get to London, and there will come another part where we'll need luck, hitching around to the M4. After that it will be plain sailing to Bristol and back up our own M5 to Base Camp.'

'And you think we can make it all before Dinner?' Squire still wanted to know.

'Who cares,' Lucan demanded, 'when there are such beautiful things to see every mile of the motorways? Look at that!' He pointed up the road to where a Lotus Elite 504 was coming down from Worcester. A fitful gleam of sun reflected back from its raked windscreen. Sleek and low on its fat, wide tyres it came lapping up the road.

'Why is it braking so hard?' Cassius asked.

'Look across the road and you'll see,' said McKlickety.

They all looked. On the far side of the motorway, high up on the bank, was a little shelf cut out like a reviewing platform to take the motorists' salutes. And perched upon it was the striped white, red and blue of a police Jaguar, watching everything that went by. The dogs all turned to Lucan.

'Well,' he said, 'today I think we'll circumnavigate the other way round. We'll go south first. It will be a little harder, but let's call it a challenge.'

Quietly the dogs slipped down the stairs of the tower and away – through the wood.

Down in the police Jaguar, P.C. Minster scowled out at the almost empty motorway. His new co-driver was P.C. Isles, and P.C. Isles was listening to Radio Two which was quite against regulations. P.C. Minster still wanted to become a Chief Constable, but with mates like P.C.

Isles beside him it looked like being an uphill struggle.

'There may be messages coming through for us,' he grumbled, 'important messages about car thieves on the move, and all we're getting is this rubbishy music.'

'At half-past seven on a Sunday morning! You must be joking,' P.C. Isles told him. 'You won't get any messages this side of midday. Everyone's fast asleep. Like we ought to be.'

'Well, we should be checking car speeds,' P.C. Minster changed his attack. 'That Lotus that's just passed was doing well over eighty.'

'Till he saw us,' said P.C. Isles firmly. 'When they see us, they all slow down. That's what we're here for, doing our duty, ain't it?'

'Those dogs may be on the move any time now,' P.C. Minster added fiercely. 'We've got to watch out for them, too. It'll be hard to see them from here if they're lying down in the back of a lorry.' P.C. Isles had heard about the events in Tewkesbury the night before. He smiled to himself. Better humour him, he thought, it would soon be breakfast.

'Yeah, there's some terrors around these days, Malc,' he said soothingly, 'but don't worry. The criminal always slips up in the end.'

Ten minutes later, still very early in the day, the Rock Dog Gang was surveying the lorry park of the south-bound station at Strensham Services. Lucan had decided that they would not eat breakfast until the Services at Gordano, or, if they were very lucky, at Leigh Delamere on the M4.

'That looks a very determined lorry,' he pointed to a Volvo F85. It had a long low body which was easy to jump up into, and there were lots of warm sacks inside.

'Let's choose that one now while no one is looking.'

They scrambled in and settled down, glad of the sacks as the wind was still rising. Very soon after they heard someone climb into the cab. Sheila risked a peep, she was a nervous passenger.

'How nice,' she reported. 'He looks a really quiet man and he has his wife and two kiddies with him.'

Odd, thought Lucan, but before he could say anything the Volvo was away.

'This is a very sharp bend. I don't remember it on the way up,' Cassius commented as they began a tight loop back underneath the M5.

'You wouldn't; we didn't come this way.' Lucan slumped down in despair.

'What's gone wrong? We haven't been going two minutes,' said McKlickety.

Lucan explained what had happened. They had turned west down that oddest, yet very early, motorway, the M50, which winds through country so wooded and lush that wild daffodils actually grow on its central reservation as if to celebrate the fact that it leads towards Wales. Not that it actually gets to Wales, but at Ross-on-Wye it turns into a dual carriageway which links up at Abergavenny with the Heads of the Valleys road where sheep live on the verges and collieries are dying on every other hill.

'It's no use,' Lucan declared crossly. 'We'll just have to thump against the cab, stop the lorry near Ross, and go back again. This is not a real motorway, it hasn't even got a Services for breakfast, and who wants to end up in the middle of Herefordshire where there's nothing but birds and trees?'

'I'll help you thump the cab,' said Khamsin eagerly. 'I enjoyed that last time.'

'Got your iron collars on, have you?' McKlickety asked

rudely. 'If you take a look at the cab you'll see it's separate from us. We could run against the end wall all day but no one would hear us in the cab. We're stuck in this until the driver decides to stop, and he's just filled up at Strensham. Probably eaten there as well.'

'I say,' Squire protested, 'that isn't true, is it, Super?'

But it was.

Lucan did his best to rally.

'He won't be going very far with his two children in the cab,' he suggested hopefully.

'Perhaps to Church,' Sheila put in brightly. 'That would be nice!'

'No one says anything about breakfast,' Squire complained, 'and back at Strensham those two girls, Lena and Sandra, would have been only too pleased to give us a bite.'

'One thing,' Lucan insisted, 'we are moving.'

No one argued about that. At a steady sixty the Volvo passed Ross at the end of the motorway and sped on along the exciting dual carriage road part of the A40. Glumly the hungry dogs watched Monmouth and the wooded hills of the Wye fall behind them.

'Where are we now?' Cassius asked. 'I mean, I'm enjoying it, it's a great ride and all that, but one does like to know when it might . . .'

'Shut up!' said McKlickety.

'I don't honestly know,' Lucan admitted. 'My owner and I only used to go on motorways and I've only seen a map that showed them, not ordinary roads. But we must be getting very close to Wales.'

'Is that good?' Khamsin asked.

'I think it's an easier place to get into than to get out of,' said Lucan cautiously. 'And I've never heard of it being very modern.'

It was a bad moment, but there was worse ahead. At Abergavenny it began to rain in the wind, great drenching gusts that soaked them as they huddled against the sides of the lorry. The Black Mountains closed around the road. At Tretower they branched off the A40 on to the A470; there were hills and more hills and dim little towns and shapeless brick villages.

The Wye had come back to them. After Pant Mawr the road topped a pass and began to slope downhill at last. The rain stopped though the wind was stronger than ever. The houses were stony and alien, the trees meagre. There was a different smell in the air.

'He's taking them to the seaside!' Lucan announced. 'Can't you smell the salt in the air?'

Everyone sniffed and caught the tang. Lucan began to brighten up.

'The seaside!' he repeated. 'Don't you remember that was one of the things we were going to experience? All humans love going there!'

'Have you ever been yourself?' McKlickety asked.

'No, but it's like a pop festival for everybody,' Lucan assured them. He was a naturally optimistic dog. Optimism is a part of being intelligent. 'This is great! I'm afraid it's not Blackpool; that's on the M55. But it will be a kind of Welsh Blackpool. We might stop some days here.'

The other dogs received all this enthusiasm quietly. It was Lucan's first failure after a run of successes and they were rather shocked.

Early in the afternoon the big Volvo ran into Aberystwyth where all the days seem perpetual afternoon. Most of the inhabitants were still drinking coffee after the Sunday roast; but over-dressed children were beginning to gather around the huge Chapels, waiting in frocks and suits for Sunday School to open. The few early visitors

were shrinking in shelters along the front, hiding from a howling gale which was lashing the promenade with pebbles and green waves. The juggernaut lorry pulled up outside Haul y Bryn boarding house, and stiffly the dogs roused themselves to jump out.

'This is it!' Lucan declared. 'The seaside where everyone goes for a fortnight each year to have fun.'

Squire cocked his ear to the furious sound of wind, water and pebbles.

'The question is,' he said, 'have we picked the right fortnight?'

'Once we've had something to eat we'll see it all differently. Let's try this café, it looks good for a bacon sandwich if we put on some really attractive tricks,' Lucan was working hard to rescue the day.

Khamsin pushed the door open and they all followed him. A sharp-nosed lady came out fast from behind the bar holding a broom.

'Cer allan oddiyma y cwn budur,' she cried.

'What did she say?' asked Squire.

'I don't even understand the language they speak here,' Lucan complained. 'The Welsh must have a language of their own to use privately.'

Khamsin tried barking at the sharp-nosed lady but she rapped his head with her broom and he went out quickly after the others.

'I don't think they're the same as the English,' Lucan explained. 'Let's try that Hot Dog stall. I never like the name but the man who's running it looks bored, so he may be interested in us.'

Eifion Hughes was a student at Aberystwyth University College who sold hot dogs in the holidays. No one was buying hot dogs in a raging gale, so when the dogs put on a five-minute show of begging, standing on heads and

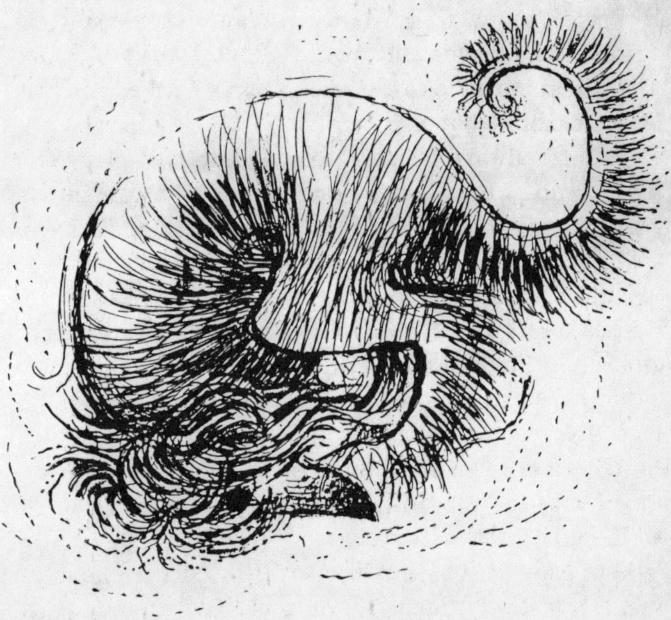

somersaulting, Eifion gave in at once and made two hot dogs for each of them, one with tropical fruit mango chutney relish and one with mustard.

'Must be rising unemployment in the circuses, I suppose,' he muttered to himself as the dogs trotted off, licking their lips.

They went down to the sea front and peered around the corner of a low wall at the ferocious waves battering against the granite walls.

'What do they do to the sea,' Khamsin asked, 'to make it so irritable?'

'It can't always be like this,' Lucan was puzzled. 'I know people often take their clothes off and walk into it.'

'You're getting muddled up with hot baths,' Sheila told him. 'No one could possibly walk into this.'

They marched along the front, keeping well away from the sea, until they came to Constitution Hill with a rack and pinion railway up its side.

'Perhaps there's a lot of fun going on up at the top,' Lucan suggested. 'Let's go up and see.'

'Where are you lot goin'?' one of the attendants demanded as they trooped into one of the little open cars which go up the railway.

'Aw, go on. Give 'em a lift,' said the other attendant. 'If you ask them for money you'll soon have them on strike for higher wages and we've got enough of that!'

Laughing at their joke, they allowed the dogs in, with a car to themselves. It began to climb, the town dropped below them and a hideous expanse of grey fretful ocean opened up to the near horizon. The wind shook the car as it climbed steadily, the wires and cogs gleaming with new oil. The attendant at the top had been warned by 'phone and was all ready to be funny.

'Welcome to Aberystwyth,' he said as the car pulled up. 'His Worship the Mayor would have been here to greet you but he's polishing his chain.'

The dogs ignored him and walked out on to the viewing-place at the top.

'So this is Aberystwyth,' said Lucan, 'at least we know where we are.'

'It's been interesting to come here but we're not going to stay long, are we?' Cassius asked.

'Perhaps there are some human fun things that don't appeal so much to dogs,' Lucan explained. 'The seaside is probably like smoking: something they enjoy but which we can't take.'

'Can we run down this hill, jumping?' Khamsin asked. 'I'd like that.'

'Race you!' Lucan challenged, and they all rushed head-long down Constitution Hill, barking to let off steam.

'There's a pick-up truck just leaving,' Cassius pointed to a van with an open back. It was the kind small farmers use to take a few milk churns to the road or one or two sheep to market. The driver had parked on the front and now he was having trouble with the choke.

'It will be a change from huge lorries that can't be stopped,' said Lucan. 'Let's take a chance on it. But get in very quietly and keep close under his rear window.'

9

Wild Wales and wilder aggro

So it was that when Mark Pritchard, who had driven his wife down for a breath of sea air on a Sunday morning, drove back into the hills again, he took six large dogs with him.

'This engine hasn't got much pull in it,' he complained as he changed down into first gear to get up Mynydd Bach.

'It's like you then, Pritchard,' retorted his wife sharply. And that set them off on a happy exchange of insults which lasted well into Pontrhydfendigaid.

For the dogs, who had eaten only two hot sausages each all day, it was a very long drive. They could hear the Pritchards nagging away behind them and for hour after hour all they could see was an endless succession of low dripping trees, stone walls and blank faced farms. Then the truck stopped.

'He's getting out to open a gate. I think it's a farm,' Squire reported.

'And I can hear several dogs,' said Khamsin. 'That means aggro, doesn't it?'

'Farm dogs!' Lucan exclaimed in disgust. 'We're getting out.'

'Couldn't we have a fight?' Khamsin suggested eagerly. 'Probably there's only two of them and they'd be tied up. We could jump on them!'

'No!' Lucan was very firm. 'Out you all get. From now on we walk. Farm dogs are the end! The utter absolute unlimited end! They only understand about six words and a lot of whistle calls, they get fleas, and they hate all other dogs. What's worse is that they're totally obedient to their owners, like slaves.'

Mark Pritchard, turning from opening his five-bar gate, was astonished to see not one but six dogs leap like a dark tide out of the back of his truck and run off down the road.

'*Dewkes Amwyll!*' he said to his wife, and his hand was shaking as he clung to the car door. 'I've just seen the pack of ghost hounds that hunted old Harry Powell over Cefn moor.'

'Oh, yes,' said Mrs Pritchard sharply, 'and I know what comes next. You'll want a tot of my cooking brandy when we get into the house to help you recover from the shock!'

They were still arguing when the pack of ghost hounds rounded the next bend in the lane and lost them for ever. The quiet of the countryside enclosed the dogs and for a time they trotted in silence. Once an owl called down by a stream, and once they heard the chug of a generator up on a hill farm, but mostly it was scents and smells that occupied their attention. After the nose-deadening petrol fumes of the pick-up truck it was all refreshing and, to most of them, new.

'I have to admit,' said McKlickety in a much milder tone than usual, 'that I like this. It reminds me of old times.'

'A country walk is grand,' Squire agreed. 'My owner

used to shoot, and I'd usually go out with him to fetch things back. A fat partridge carried back over short stubble, now, I'd always enjoy that. The trouble with the country is that it goes on so long and you can never control it.'

'How are you getting on, Sheila?' Lucan asked the old Labrador. She had been very silent since they had left the van.

'I don't complain,' she said, 'but my arthritis gives me a very nasty jip sometimes. I'm supposed to keep off my left foreleg as much as I can.'

'How far do you think we are from Base Camp?' asked Cassius. 'I'm not grumbling, you know, it's very interesting walking here at the back of nowhere, but I just wondered when we might . . .'

'About a hundred miles at a guess,' said Lucan shortly; his coat was warm and he was a tireless walker, but the country bored him. With Sheila's arthritis he could see them taking five days to get back to Strensham and the Base Camp.

'We'll find a warm barn,' McKlickety said encouragingly, 'and then I'll see if I can snatch us a couple of fat hens for dinner.'

'To eat raw!' said Sheila faintly. 'I don't know that I could ever manage anything raw. What I would like now is a nice piece of cake.'

Lucan groaned inside himself at the responsibility of looking after a whole gang, some of them much weaker than himself, most of them much less intelligent. The trouble all came from depending on lifts.

'A Rock Gang rocks along with whatever comes up,' he said firmly. 'If it's windy, night time, and the middle of Wales, well, we'll just enjoy it for what it is and roll along with it. With McKlickety around we'll never starve, and it's not a cold night. Sooner or later we'll hit a main road and get a lift on a milk lorry. They go for miles. And at least we've got away from that policeman that seemed to keep chasing after us.'

For another hour they trudged on, and now Sheila was in real difficulties with her arthritis and Khamsin had a thorn in his foot. Lucan was just deciding to stop at the next farm when they heard a motor of some sort coming up behind them.

'All into the ditch,' Lucan called, 'the lane's narrow here. If only we could hitch lifts with thumbs like humans do.'

The vehicle coming up behind them looked like a small Land Rover with a canvas top. It was being driven very fast for the type of road it was on. As it bounced by, Lucan caught a mixed smell of old objects that he felt he should remember and heard an exclamation from the driver. The brakes went on hard and it pulled up just ahead of them.

'Please, let it be him!' hoped Lucan. The driver got out and turned back to meet them.

'Lord bless my boots if it ain't you lot again,' he said. 'Now if that doesn't take some beating!'

As Lucan had hoped, it was Ben!

The dogs gathered in the circle of the vehicle's head-lights and looked at him in amazement.

'Come on, let's show enthusiasm,' called Lucan, who was genuinely at least as much pleased as he was surprised. He, Khamsin and Squire, with varying degrees of bounce and vigour, flung themselves at Ben to give him a good licking. Dogs like to lick humans according to how salty their skin is. Ben's skin was very salty so they welcomed him thoroughly. As usual he talked aloud to them, but this did not immediately clear up the mystery of his arrival.

'Right, right, give over,' he shouted, pushing them

back but actually enjoying it all. 'Just you tell me what you're doing out here five miles from Llangammarch Wells, when I last saw you on the village green at Earls Priestly?'

But of course the dogs could not tell him.

'Want a lift in my Mini Moke, do you?' Ben asked.

Lucan risked nodding. In the dark Ben would never be sure of what he had seen.

'Pile in, then. I don't know if there's room for all of you. There's two more of you than I saw last time. Oops a daisy, lady,' he said as he helped Sheila into the rear part of the car.

That was not easy. The rear part of the Moke held two big packing cases. Their tops were open and covered with rough sacking. A jumble of hard angular objects and curved shapes could be felt through this as the dogs scrambled to find places. As Cassius tried to sit on top of one case the hidden objects sank down and there was the unmistakable clank of metal on crockery.

'Cripes,' Ben exclaimed, 'there's twenty thousand quid's worth of stolen goods in there. I'm not carting it

around for a pooch with a punched-up face to smash. Get off, you brute!'

As he pushed Cassius off his perch there was an ominous jingle of broken glass from inside the case. Lucan noted it all and sniffed carefully. The 'old' smell was certainly coming from the cases and it was all starting to add up.

When they were all packed in, Lucan and Khamsin in the front, the rest lying or sitting in the back, Ben took a last look round the lane to satisfy himself that no human had been with the dogs, got back in and started up the Mini Moke.

It was just like driving in the open air; there was a canvas roof and canvas and plastic side screens that buttoned into studs on the chassis, but the air whistled in everywhere and the springing gave you a clear idea of the exact surface of the lane. At first Ben concentrated on driving, saying nothing. Then he risked a glance at Lucan, just as Lucan was risking a glance at him. Both turned hurriedly away again to stare at the brief world of hedges, rowan bushes and scrubby oaks which the headlights lit up.

'Just what is this?' Ben asked in a tone halfway between crossness and laughing. 'Just what's going on here? Still, I suppose I picked you up; I could have gone on and left you, couldn't I? But you're a right odd lot, you are. I tell you what you are, you're a gang! You're Lucan's Gang, the Terrors of the Welsh Border. Crippen! I've thought of something, what if you're police decoys with radio tracking beacons?'

Sweating freely, Ben pulled the Moke into a gateway and began to run his hands over all the dogs, particularly around their collars and Squire's huge ears, looking for a miniature radio beacon.

'Give him a few licks,' Lucan ordered. 'I said a few!' he snapped as Khamsin covered Ben's face with wet. 'Now roll on your backs, wag your tails and whimper a bit. Make him feel guilty. I'll tell you later what he's looking for.'

'No, I can't chuck you out again right up here,' said Ben as he completed the search. 'Anyway, it was a daft idea of mine; I must be getting nervy. Cool it, Ben Short. You're letting the job get you down.'

He started up the engine again and drove on.

'It's not very comfortable back here,' McKlickety reported. 'What has Ben got in these cases?'

'Antiques,' Lucan told him. 'Old things that are very valuable. I've seen them on television.'

'Antiques are nice,' Sheila was warming to Ben as her arthritic leg improved. 'Does Ben collect them?'

'In a way,' Lucan told her, 'but not the right way. I'll explain later.'

They drove around Builth Wells, missing the town by taking a tangle of narrow lanes. Ben knew that bored policemen on night duty will stop anything that moves.

And then disaster struck.

'This is it,' said Ben in a desperately worried voice, 'a police check with sniffer dogs and me with two cases of nicked antiques in the back.' He looked over his shoulder, wondering whether to risk a reverse and turn, but it was pub emptying time and there were five other cars behind him.

'Ready for action!' Lucan warned the dogs. 'Real aggro this time.'

The Moke pulled up, a policeman left the car in front, which he had been examining, and came over to them.

'Do you mind getting out of your car, please, sir?' he asked courteously. 'This is an official check point of Powys police. Could I see your licence, please?'

As Ben pulled out his licence, a police dog-handler came up the road towards them. Straining on a short leash he had a Keeshond called Tagger. Keeshonds are a big, woolly, nervous breed of dog. They often have a very keen sense of smell. Tagger could sniff out anything.

'Don't hurt him,' Lucan told the others, 'but give him a nasty fright and make a terrible noise. Give it all you've got!'

As the Keeshond came up, the policeman examining Ben's licence was just about to explain the search when the Moke erupted dogs. Khamsin, Cassius and McKlickety got hold of Tagger and threw him over, snarling wickedly as they did so. Squire jumped out, stood on the Keeshond, put back his head and howled. Lucan grabbed the handler's wrist and made him drop the leash. Sheila barked for all she was worth.

In the semi-darkness the confusion was complete.

'Quick, help me, they've got Tagger down!' the handler called to the other policemen.

'For Pete's sake, what have you got, a travelling menagerie?' the first policeman asked Ben. Car horns sounded behind.

'Hurry up,' a voice called, 'we've got five cars waiting here and one of them's the High Sheriff's.'

All the time the dogs kept up their babble of barks, snarls and howls, with the Keeshond Tagger now howling louder than any of them.

'Right!' said the first policeman. 'Call your dogs off, get 'em back in the van and drive on! Here's your licence. Next time keep them under check. It could be an offence.'

'Sorry, officer,' said Ben, eager relief brimming in his voice. 'I'll do that. Down, get down! Back with you!' and he waded into the dogfight with his boots.

‘Drop everything,’ Lucan ordered, ‘back into the van, but let’s have even more noise.’

The Keeshond, released, jumped to its feet and ran headlong down the road.

‘We’ll get no work out of him tonight,’ his handler complained. ‘He’s a very highly strung dog, very sensitive!’

‘I’m really sorry about that,’ said Ben. ‘Mine are usually quiet as lambs. I can’t understand it.’

‘Drive on,’ the first policeman shouted over the uproar.

Ben dived back into the Moke and shot off, passing a line of cars waiting to come the other way. The dog noises ended abruptly.

‘We made him bite the bullet,’ Khamsin panted happily. ‘That was the best bit of aggro since we started out.’

‘I pushed him over first,’ Cassius claimed. ‘I mean, you all helped, it was wonderful team work, but I was what I suppose you’d call the hitman.’

McKlickety, who had really done all the rough stuff, sat back on the packing cases and said nothing. Sheila sniffed scornfully and said that it would have been a poor show if six of them couldn’t deal with one Keeshond.

‘I always believe that they’re crossed with sheep, anyway,’ she finished, ‘because some people mix Keeshond fur with nylon and knit it into cardigans for ladies. My blind person had one but it all fell to bits.’

‘You flippin’ wonderful set of dogs!’ Ben kept saying. ‘You blinking wonderful bunch of beauties! I’ll never forget this. So help me I won’t. And stop me into a muddy puddle if I run another load of this junk over the Border for Jerry Joiner while he sits back and I take the risks. You’ve saved me, you dogs have. Pulled me right out of it. And I’d take an oath you all know what you’ve done, by the look on your faces!’

'He sounds excited,' Squire commented. 'Perhaps you can tell us now what we've all been up to. I'm getting a bit old for this sort of thing.'

So, while Ben kept stroking him and scratching him behind his right ear, Lucan told the others about the hidden garage by the motorway and what was in the two packing cases.

'Has Ben stolen these antiques himself?' Squire asked disapprovingly.

'I don't think so,' Lucan said; and he explained that Ben was probably being used by the real criminals to pick up valuables that had been stolen in Saturday night burglaries from Welsh antique shops and country houses. He was bringing these down to the hidden garage and from there they could be taken down the motorways to any handy port and shipped off to America almost before the police had a description of them.

'Now what do you think we ought to do?' Lucan asked them when he'd finished. 'It's your decision; we're a gang.'

'Nuffin',' said Khamsin immediately. 'Go on helping Ben. I think he's great! We'll be dog smugglers.'

'Leave them to get on with it,' McKlickety sounded very certain: 'I don't like it when people bother me, so I don't believe in bothering people.'

'I know very little,' Sheila began, in that firm tone of voice which means that people think they know a great deal, 'but I can tell right from wrong. Anything which you steal must be wrong. So we should never have interfered when the police were trying to find it. I wish now that I hadn't barked; I felt very foolish at the time. But Lucan ordered us to, and he's our leader.'

'Yes, that's true,' Lucan admitted, giving Ben's hand a lick to calm him down. 'I'm responsible, but all of you must decide what we do next. What do you think, Cassius?' he asked the Boxer encouragingly.

'Oh my,' said Cassius unhappily. 'Decisions! Decisions! This just isn't my line. I never know what to do. I just try to be kind to everyone.'

'And look where that's got you!' said McKlickety meanly.

'How about Squire?' Lucan asked quickly to avoid trouble.

'I believe in fun,' said Squire heavily, 'but I believe in property, and it's no fun having your property stolen. I don't want to get Ben in trouble. He's a great lad. He may be quite a musician for all I can tell but we have to lead him away from crime. I say we should catch the real criminals who put him up to all this and get these packing cases to the police.'

'Agreed,' said Lucan. 'We'll start working on it!'

As Ben drove carefully over the Malverns and back to the hideout with his loot, the dogs debated how they could make sure that he never drove a cargo like that again.

'That's my last trip,' Ben said rather uncertainly as he drove through the bushes into the hidden clearing. He groped his way into the dark shed, leaving the dogs in the Moke. It was the chance Lucan had been waiting for.

The car keys hung from the ignition with a broad loop of leather dangling from them. Quickly and carefully Lucan pushed his paw into the loop, tightened it with a little twist, then pulled the starting key out of the ignition.

'What are you doing, Super Boss?' Khamsin asked. 'Ben needs that to make it work.'

'I know all about that,' Lucan replied mysteriously.

'That's clever,' said Cassius. 'Now Ben won't be able to drive around getting himself into trouble.'

'I don't know about that,' Squire warned. 'It's easy

enough to buy new ignition keys. My owner was always losing them.'

'Isn't it a lovely moon?' Lucan tried to change the subject. 'Perhaps we could chase a few rabbits before we go to sleep.'

'My arthritis is better,' said Sheila doubtfully, 'but still not right.'

Squire was even more anxious to avoid activity. He hated hunting, especially if you actually caught something.

'Hello, hello,' he said brightly, 'what's this Ben has left on the seat?'

'Money,' reported McKlickety. 'One note and a silver bit. They fell out when he was getting his keys.'

As Lucan looked at the five pound note and the fifty pence lying there on the Moke's battered driving seat, a memory bell chimed in his head. Petrol costs money, and if he had his way the gang was going to need petrol.

'Khamsin,' he said, 'you've got a dry mouth. Pick up the note and bring it along to Base Camp. Cassius, you carry the fifty pence piece. It won't matter if that gets wet. We've saved Ben from the police tonight and if we use this money wisely, all work together and ask questions later, much later, we'll probably save Ben from himself, which is more important.'

'Much more,' Sheila agreed. 'My old owner always used to say that a day when you help someone to help themselves is a day when the sun shines.'

'Was that why she chucked you out into the cold?' McKlickety asked, as meanly as ever.

'Time for sleep,' Lucan said quickly. 'Pick that money up like I told you. Quick! Ben's just coming back from that smelly old shed.'

When Ben came out from emptying the garage the

clearing was deserted. That was when he found the Moke's ignition key was missing.

In the dark, with thick leaf mould on the worn tarmac, it was not easy to search and Ben was very tired. There were only six hours to go before he would be awake again tending the cows. After a few minutes he gave up, and pushed the light little car bodily into the garage. He forgot to lock up, wearily mounted his Triumph and drove unsteadily away across the field towards his home. Up in the tower room Lucan half heard the engine in his sleep and smiled to himself.

10

An all-time first

'What do we do today?' Khamsin asked when he woke up at seven-thirty next morning.

'Food!' said Squire, even before he was properly awake. 'A good square meal, that's what we do first.'

So Lucan led them all down through the woods, barking at grey squirrels to relieve their feelings, and into the Strensham Motorway Services. They were in luck. Middlesborough had been playing Bristol City that weekend and a coach load of Middlesborough supporters had had to leave in a hurry. The wastebins were full of cold sausages and chips and the dogs were soon tucking in.

'I told you the motorways were the place for good food,' Lucan reminded them contentedly.

'These are meat, are they?' Khamsin was chewing a sausage with a puzzled expression on his face.

'Bound to be,' said Lucan. 'Now listen, Gang. This afternoon Ben and Kevin are both riding at motocross on Dymock Common, so they'll be out of our way and Ben should be out of mischief. I've got his car keys and that means we can start driving lessons!'

Thc others looked at him and then looked at each other.

'Dogs can't drive,' said McKlickety flatly.

'One can't, but six could,' Lucan insisted.

They lay digesting their sausages and Lucan's new idea as the morning rush of lorries swirled by.

'I don't have to do anything, do I?' Sheila pursued. 'It's a chilly morning and what my arthritis needs is a nice warm electric fire and the steam from my old lady's twin-tub washing machine. Then if I'm lucky she'll notice my limp and bandage me up. There's nothing to touch a bit of old flannel for an arthritic leg. I may come along with you this evening and then again I may not. It all depends on my leg.'

The old dog padded off towards Inglenook Cottage where her sponsor was just starting the Monday wash.

'Huh!' said Khamsin. 'I don't rate women, and I don't reckon there's much place for them in a really wild gang.'

'She has the right idea about sponsors,' Lucan told him. 'We're going to have a sponsor-cultivating morning. Work hard on them. Give them a good time – tricks, affection and lots of attention. This afternoon I'll want you all helping me down at the Mini Moke. Tomorrow is going to be one of the all-time firsts.'

'Well, you can count me out for a start,' said McKlickety. 'My owner's going ratting at the Home Farm.'

'Your *what* is going ratting?' snapped Lucan.

'I said "my owner",' McKlickety replied defiantly. 'I like him and I like working on a National Trust stately home. It's as good a Rock as your motors.'

'Right,' said Lucan soothingly. 'Let's make a bargain. This afternoon we all practise on the car and this evening you take us all round your stately home. Agreed? Then we can judge which is the most Rock.'

McKlickety was trapped. They agreed to meet at the clearing around midday, then they divided and set off to work on their sponsors. Lucan trotted over to Ben's farm to help with the cows. He was sharing Ben's elevenses in a sunny corner of the rick yard when Kevin came pedalling hard up the lane on his bicycle.

'Why aren't you at school, Kev?' Ben asked in his big brother voice.

'Jerry Joiner came past at morning break and said to meet him at twelve o'clock sharp on the green with our gear. He'll have the bikes and we can get over to Dymock early for a practice. They've done my tank and mudguards in fibreglass now and Jerry says it's taken pounds off the weight!'

Kevin could hardly speak for excitement and puffing.

'And what about my cows?' Ben wanted to know.

'Jerry said to say he met your boss in Tewkesbury this morning and Mr Higman says it's all right with him. He'll take over. Jerry's fixed everything!'

'And what about your schooling? Don't tell me Jerry Joiner's fixed your headmistress. That I don't believe.'

‘Aw, Ben, don’t be like that! It’s only this once. I was thinking all through arithmetic this morning about how I ought to take that skid pan corner at Knott’s elm. I’ve been leaning in too much and braking down. Next time I’m going to try leaning out and accelerating. What do you think?’

And in no time the two brothers were deep into tactics and Ben had forgotten all about Kevin’s school. They tucked Kevin’s push bike away in a barn and both got on to Ben’s Triumph Thunderbird. That was another blow for Lucan as he had been working out how to hitch a lift on the pillion all morning. As the old engine roared into life Kevin glanced round and caught Lucan trying to look as if he didn’t care.

‘Here, boy!’ he called, and patted the worn saddle in front of him.

‘That dog hasn’t got a crash helmet,’ Ben protested, but Lucan could tell he didn’t mind. Quickly he leaped up between them and sat squashed sideways with Kevin holding him tight as they swung off down the lane.

It was a memory mile for Lucan as they swooped round bends, feeling every rut of the lane, sunshine and slip stream soaking into his fur and the fresh air forcing itself down his open mouth. Much too soon they pulled up by the council houses and Lucan jumped down to wait while the boys rushed off for their gear.

Happiness and gloom chased each other round Lucan’s mind. With a bit of luck and some firm planning he might just manage to drive a motor car, but now he knew how terrific it was to be on a motor bike, and with just his four paws he could never hope to drive one of those.

Loaded down with leathers, mittens, padded jackets and boots, the boys came hurrying out of the house, and

Lucan scrambled up to follow them.

'No good coming with us this time, Lucan lad,' Ben called. 'Jerry Joiner don't like dogs. Says they leave hair on his seat cushions.'

And with this they were off in a roar of splendid noise. For a moment Lucan was so cross he almost gave up. But he was very keen to meet Jerry Joiner and it was a lovely day so he settled down to a steady run. Five minutes later he was at the Green just as a big grey Volvo drove up with its lights gleaming feebly in the spring sunshine. Behind, on a trailer, were perched Ben's 125 cc Kawasaki, grass green and sky blue, and Kevin's 75 cc Yamaha in black and white checks.

From a distance, Lucan watched as a small red-faced man in a camel hair coat got out of the Volvo and walked round to lean on the bonnet and talk to Ben. While Kevin was busy stowing gear in the boot, Lucan sneaked quietly across, scrabbled under the car and wriggled cautiously forward until he could hear what Ben and Jerry were saying. They were having a row.

'Aw, Jerry!' Ben grumbled. 'Do I have to? I reckon I'm due for a break.'

'Most people that see you driving around on these expensive bikes of mine would say you were getting the breaks already, and plenty of them!' Jerry said meaningfully. 'Anyway, I'm taking you off the Wales collection run for a bit. The police have seen you. Someone else will ship the loot in next Sunday.'

'Oh thanks, Jerry!' Ben sounded so weak that Lucan felt quite ashamed of him.

'Don't thank me. You'll still earn your keep. I'm putting you on the run to Ellesmere Port tomorrow night.'

'Ellesmere Port!' Ben sounded frightened this time. 'That's up near Liverpool. It'll take me all night, and delivering stolen stuff to a dock area is dangerous. The cops are everywhere!'

'The police never expect to find cases of valuable antiques on oil tankers,' Jerry said smoothly. 'You'll be safer than houses and it'll make a nice change to the back lanes. Start at midnight, deliver at Dock Gate 12 at three in the morning. You'll make it back for milking time.'

'Count me out, Jerry. It's too dangerous.' Ben's voice was sullen. There was a pause.

'Kevin,' Jerry raised his voice. 'Come round here a minute, will you?'

Lucan watched Kevin's feet move round the Volvo to join the other feet.

'How's the bike going, lad?' Jerry asked in an extra friendly tone.

'Well,' Kevin began, 'my chain's been slackening. I think the tensioner's bent again.'

'Tensioner's going again, eh?' said Jerry meaningfully, his shoes turning to Ben rather than his brother. 'Well, never mind, I reckon we ought to try a gold-anodised, light-alloy swing-arm next time. Of course it's all money,' here he prodded Ben's boot with his brogue, 'but there's plenty of that around. Leave it with me and we'll see what we can do before your next race. You're a great little rider, Kev, a great little rider. I'm proud of you. Next July you'll be the tops.'

Kevin said nothing, but he stood up straighter.

'Check the bikes up on the trailer, will you, Kev?' Jerry asked. 'Ben and me will be with you in a minute if you want any help.'

'I'll be OK, Jerry, and thanks a lot.' Kevin went round to the back to check the two bikes. Ben watched him in his leather jeans, shoulder pads and helmet, trudging like a miniature Martian across the grass. Jerry watched Ben. Underneath the car Lucan watched their feet, and listened.

'He's a great kid, that brother of yours,' Jerry went on. 'Motocross means a lot to him. It might hit the kid hard if I had to withdraw my backing.'

'Yeah, all right.' By the tone of his voice Lucan knew that Ben had given in to help his younger brother. 'I'll drive the Moke tomorrow night.'

'I knew you wouldn't let me down,' said Jerry Joiner. 'Drive carefully. There's a pricey bit of flash silverware in one of those two cases. Worth all the other stuff put together if my dealer in the States can get a fair price for it.'

'What's that, Jerry?' Ben asked.

'It's only about two feet high but it's five hundred years old, the Llantyr Abbey cross. Supposed to be the only one that survived when Henry VIII bust up the monasteries.' Jerry laughed. 'It's been lying around doing nothing in a Welsh country house since 1550 so I got one of my best cat burglars to swipe it. Time it got into circulation again!'

Lucan scrambled out from under the car and headed back across the fields to the tower. He was a very worried dog. Jerry Joiner was an even nastier rogue than he had been expecting. If Ben were to be rescued from a spell in Borstal it was vital for the Gang to drive the Moke.

He nipped quickly up the tower stairs to collect the ignition key. Sheila was sitting waiting for him and looking rather guilty.

'Hello!' he said. 'I thought you were doing the wash with your old lady.'

'Well, I was,' Sheila admitted, 'and I'm just on my way back to air the clothes and perhaps have a sit in front of the coal fire. But I thought I'd look in to show willing and ask if there was anything I could do to help. Not that I ever wanted to drive myself, but a spin on a sunny afternoon with the heater full on is just my cup of tea.'

'We're not all made to be pioneers,' Lucan agreed, 'but I'll tell you what you could do that would be useful. I don't want you actually to steal anything, but two soft hats, a pair of leather gloves and an old raincoat would be a great help.'

'I won't promise anything, but I'll keep an eye open,' said Sheila. 'Good luck!' and she limped off down the stairs.

'Good for her,' Lucan thought as he scampered down to the secret clearing with the precious key ring in his mouth.

The other four dogs were waiting patiently for him. They had all had a good morning with their sponsors and a tasty lunch so Lucan felt self-righteous.

'It's going to take hard work and discipline,' he warned them, 'and we'll never get into a book of records because no one will believe it; but driving a car is the most important thing anyone can ever do, so we're going to do it. Then we can go anywhere and enjoy everything. We'll be mobile!'

'Daredevil dog drivers!' shouted Khamsin, and he bounded around the clearing. 'Watch me burn the road up!'

'If he thinks he's going to do the driving,' thought Lucan, 'he's got a surprise coming to him.'

Ben had forgotten to lock the garage and Squire was a heavy dog with a good push to his shoulder, so they managed easily. There was the Mini Moke waiting for them, loaded with stolen valuables. Lucan remembered the silver cross and determined grimly to give Jerry Joiner his come-uppance.

'It's facing the wrong way,' said Khamsin. 'What do we do?'

'You keep quiet and get inside,' Lucan told him firmly.

Once he was seated at the wheel of the Mini Moke, Lucan set them all to their tasks. He was going to turn the ignition key with the leather loop and sit on the seat to steer the car with his forepaws. The other dogs would have to stay crowded together on the floor. Squire was in charge of the brake and McKlickety of the accelerator, Cassius would brace his back against the seat and press the clutch when they had to change gear. The gear lever itself was the hardest of all to manipulate and the only reason Lucan gave it to Khamsin was because he had a high shoulder to heave against it.

'Ideally,' said Lucan, 'a car for dogs would work by pressing buttons, but there's no market for them yet. Now! Attention, and do just what I say.'

He twisted the ignition key and there was a cough. He

twisted again and there was another cough, but still no comfortable engine sound.

'My old owner always used to pull something when he wanted to start,' Squire suggested. 'It always went then.'

'Of course, stupid me!' said Lucan. 'The choke,' and he pulled the choke button out with his teeth.

Lucan twisted the ignition again. This time it started perfectly. 'Clutch!' Cassius pressed it.

'Accelerator!' McKlickety pressed. The Moke and the five dogs all shivered together.

'Gear over hard to me,' said Lucan. 'Hard!' he called urgently as Khamsin heaved desperately up over the bridge to get into reverse. 'Now back.' The lever fell into place.

'Release the clutch gently!'

Cassius's paw slipped. The Moke shot into reverse and backed full tilt out of the elder bushes into the clearing. Desperately Lucan turned the wheel and they reversed in a tight circle. Lucan decided to get this bit right before they did anything more complicated. At least he could handle the wheel, the steering was very light. They made fifteen circuits backwards with the engine revving fiercely, then stalled as McKlickety lost interest in the accelerator and tried to look out.

'We'll try again,' said Lucan. 'Team on red alert! Clutch! Gear forward and away from me. Forward!' he shouted as poor Khamsin struggled to get his weight in the right place. 'Great! Now we're in first and we can go ahead for a change.'

'I liked going backwards,' said Khamsin.

'Yes, but it's not useful on motorways,' Lucan told him. 'We've got to be practical. If we're going to save Ben we've got to drive forwards.'

They settled down to an intense day. The clearing was a

perfect practice area. If they hit the bushes the Moke was only scratched. If they rammed a heap of gravel all they did was stall. Some time in the early afternoon Lucan persuaded Khamsin that the key control post was at the clutch.

'You mean I'm in charge of everything?'

'Life and death!' Lucan assured him.

'Geeee!'

In his place at the gear lever Cassius proved to be brilliant. He hunched, rammed and pushed his way up and down the gears with uncanny skill. Soon they were moving easily from first to third and back down again. Reverse was still difficult, and McKlickety was much too hard on the accelerator. To make up for it, Squire was ferocious on the brake pedal. Lucan bumped his nose twice on the windscreen because he could not fit into the safety belt. The other dogs did not mind this too much as they resented his being up there with all the views, while they slaved away below the dashboard.

Finally he tried out the lights, then reversed neatly back into the elder bushes, where he hid the car keys on a low branch. All four dogs felt very pleased with themselves. Cassius in particular was quite changed by the confidence he had gained gunning the gears.

'Now we have to catch up on our tea,' Squire insisted.

11

Culture-Rock

A clear double rainbow arced over them as they made their way cheerfully to Strensham Services, and all the evening birds seemed to be singing for them personally.

Ben must have been saying kind things about them to his girl friends because Sandra brought out a whole tray full of meaty goodies for them, and much too big a plate of cold chips. Heavily they jogged back to Base Camp, where Sheila was waiting at the door. She was sitting proudly beside a soft tweed gardening hat, a sou'wester, a dark blue plastic mac and a pair of black leather gardening gauntlets.

'It's my old lady,' she reported affectionately. 'Of course I haven't asked her in so many words, but she never throws anything away and I'm beginning a regular Spring Cleaning. She won't know the place when I've finished with it, I'll have it so comfy. Three trips this lot took me.'

With much scuffling and tugging they got Lucan into the raincoat, the sou'wester and gauntlets. Then he sat up on his haunches and turned sideways to the Gang. They inspected him carefully.

'Remarkable!' said Squire. 'Behind the flaps of the

Moke at three metres I'd take you for a hippy in a rainstorm.'

'We're going to make it,' Lucan assured them.

'Ain't no one going to stop us,' Khamsin agreed.

'Help me out of these,' said Lucan, 'and stow them upstairs. You've done a great job, Sheila. Now this is Culture evening, and McKlickety is going to take us round our very first Stately Home to see if it is as much of a Rock thing as driving a car.'

'Don't expect too much, will you?' McKlickety warned.

'Everyone goes round them these days,' said Lucan, 'and they charge as much as a cinema. I bet they're the tops!'

The sun was just sinking over the Malverns as the Rock Dog Gang trouped up to the stables of Kings Priestly House. On the splendid Garden Front the windows were gleaming with reflected light and the pillars were rosy with sunset colours, but here at the back of the house the shadows were gathering under the lime trees, and the only sounds were a thrush singing and horses' hooves clobbing on the cobbles in the riding stables. Secure behind a hundred burglar alarms and cosy in their luxurious attic flats, the National Trust staff were enjoying their evening television.

'Nice place they've got here,' Squire commented.

'I can't hear music yet,' complained Khamsin, 'so it can't be very loud.'

'We don't know for sure that they put much music on,' McKlickety sounded apologetic. 'Nick lives in a little cottage right across the park. I never heard much.'

'If they haven't got music how do they get people paying to come in?' Khamsin asked aggressively. 'There'd better be some jumping if there's no music.'

They made their way through the outbuildings, all carefully preserved for visitors to examine, but the dogs found them shabby, though Squire liked the stables.

'Where's the action?' Khamsin demanded. He led them through an open side door in the laundry into the servants' hall, and so up the back stairs into the Marble Hall: two hundred and thirty years old, twenty metres high and mellow with the dying western light.

'Nuffin'!' Khamsin declared. The absolute silence subdued them all. Portraits of dead Priestlys looked down from delicately-painted plaster walls, all swags and rococo swirls; the inlaid wooden staircase swept up in a double curve into the hushed floors above.

'I never promised anything,' said McKlickety defensively.

'Humans must enjoy all this or they wouldn't pay,' said Lucan, 'we ought to try to understand it.'

'I'm hungry,' said Khamsin.

'Well, this is the dining-room,' called Cassius from the door on the left. Quite unaware of the pitfalls they were accidentally avoiding, the other dogs followed him into a long room with a terracotta and cream coloured ceiling and a pink carpet woven specially on the private looms of the Kings of France.

'Let's see if they've left any food on that table,' Khamsin suggested.

'There are certainly enough plates,' said Squire hopefully.

The table was set, fully laid, for thirty-six people, with Meissen china, silver-gilt cutlery and Waterford glass, worth, in all, about £200,000. It was something with which the National Trust was taking no chances.

'I could jump from here,' Khamsin offered, and he did, over a frail rope barrier, plump! with all four heavy feet on to the pink roses of the carpet.

With a strident rattle the burglar alarms began to ring, set off by the web of delicate wiring under the carpet. Seven miles away, by automatic connection, another alarm began to ring in Worcester Police Station. In three great bounds Khamsin leaped nervously across the room and set off another system of alarms.

'Help!' he called. 'They've got me!'

'They haven't got anybody yet,' Lucan said crossly, 'but they soon will do if we don't get out of here. It's a police trap, specially set up to catch stray dogs. After me, Gang!'

Upstairs in their warm flats the National Trust custodians snapped off their T.V. sets, trampled on their coffee

cups, and came hurrying to defend their treasures. Following Lucan, the Gang ran through the Library, the Picture Gallery, the Drawing-Room, the Octagonal Boudoir and the China Room. In each of the five rooms they set off another burglar alarm. Chimes of horrid bells could be heard right across the park. Worcester Police Station, which had been going to send one police car, hurriedly dispatched six. At the wheel of one of them, diverted from motorway patrol, P.C. Malcolm Minster sat, eager for action.

The dogs came panting full circle out of the China Room back into the Marble Hall. Upstairs voices sounded:

'Who's there?'

'Stop!'

One middle-aged lady custodian, who had been watching a T.V. serial about the police, quavered:

'We have guns here, and will not hesitate to open fire!'

As the lights sprang on from thirty chandeliers the dogs scampered down into the servants' hall and out through the laundry side-door. More voices could be heard approaching from the Coachman's Lodge so they hurried out through the stable doors, across a brief lawn and into the blackthorn bushes. Here two nightingales had been roused by the burglar alarms and began to sing competitively in liquid notes.

'I knew it couldn't be all boring,' said Lucan.

'Was all that for us?' Khamsin asked.

'For you really,' McKlickety told him. 'After all, you started it!'

'Now we're really living!' Khamsin declared.

Keeping to the woods they made their way back towards Base Camp, seeing, from far off, the flashing lights of six police cars rushing to the House up four separate drives to cut off the escaping criminals.

Interviewing the custodians for clues, P.C. Minster pounced eagerly upon one lady's report that she had seen 'several fierce dogs rushing away'.

'That's them!' he declared. 'Do you think you can describe them, Madam?'

'Alsatians,' he was told, which was not at all what he wanted to hear. But one stable girl said that she too had seen the dogs 'and they were all different sizes'.

P.C. Minster reported this to his Detective Sergeant:

'You can depend on it, it's the same lot that were active last week in Bristol,' he added.

The Detective Sergeant had heard about P.C. Minster and his obsession with dogs.

'Bristol's forty miles away,' he snapped.

'They move fast,' said P.C. Minster confidently. 'The same gang broke up a peaceful music concert at Tewkesbury a few evenings ago. That's ten miles from here.'

The Detective Sergeant decided to humour him but to put in a report to the Police Medical Officer.

'Rest assured,' he said soothingly, 'we will follow all possible leads.'

Back in his austere police flat P.C. Minster got on the 'phone. He had a feeling that he was not getting official support and that it was time those Bosker sisters were brought in. They knew what he was up against.

When the phone rang, in the back living-room of Beacon House, Julie and Fran were watching the show jumping on television, spotting the horses they had seen at the Badminton Trials last year. The room was thick with Julie's cigarette smoke, and Fran's bronchitis was bad; but Julie still had her leg in plaster so Fran had to answer the 'phone.

'Oh dear!' she called to her sister. 'It's that young policeman that was so angry. He thinks he's found those wicked dogs of ours up in Worcestershire. Says they're causing an upset and wants us to come up and help identify them. Shall I put him off?'

Julie had just drunk two tots of what she called 'the real stuff', which was gin and blackcurrant juice, so she was in the mood for battle.

'Put him off?' she roared. 'Not on your life! Tell him we'll be up there as soon as . . . when can we get Old Jeff in to look after the dogs for us, Fran?'

'Not till tomorrow afternoon, Jule.'

'Tell him tomorrow afternoon, then.'

'But how will we get there, Jule? You're not fit to drive.'

'In the Austin Cambridge, of course, and you'll drive,'

Julie snarled.

'Oh Jule! I haven't driven since Father died.'

'Tell him, tomorrow, and stop nattering. They're having this very funny race between camels and horses and you're missing it! I mean to be in at the death with those dogs.'

Reluctantly Fran Bosker promised P.C. Minster that they would be up the motorway to see him the very next afternoon at two o'clock.

'Thank you, ma'am,' said P.C. Minster. 'I think I can assure you that the net is closing in!'

12

Mobile at last

When Lucan uncurled from sleep next morning he thought that the net was closing in as well. But it was his own net he was thinking about. He did not know exactly what P.C. Minster was up to, but he was fully aware of the war that was going on between the Gang and the constable. His own plan depended very much on having P.C. Minster around, and the first thing he did, after stretching his legs, was to climb up to the battlements to see if the police car was sitting on its reviewing base, guarding the motorway. Disappointingly it was not. But no matter, Lucan thought, that policeman can be relied on to turn up somewhere.

Basically Lucan was a very good-natured dog. When bad things happened to him or to his friends he would fight back, but, unlike P.C. Minster or Julie Bosker, he did not waste whole days plotting the ruin of his enemies. Just now he wanted to help Ben out of an ugly tangle, but what really filled Lucan's mind and made him stand tiptoe with happiness on the battlements of the Tower was the thought of the Gang gaining the freedom of the roads and actually driving themselves, instead of depending on lifts. Lucan shook himself with the sheer tingling pleasure of achievement, and said it to himself: The first dog driver in Britain!

He barked loudly, which was something he rarely did.

'Wake up!' he called to the others. 'This is driving day. It's just beginning to rain which is perfect for us. Hurry off down to the Service Station for a quick breakfast and see if you can bring a snack back with you. It's going to be a long day.'

The idea of food always got them on the move and the five were soon off down the hill.

This settled, Lucan turned to more serious matters. For the success of his Ben-saving plan he needed to know exactly where Jerry Joiner's house lay. From what Ben had told the group that night, coming back from Tewkesbury in the fog, he knew it was called Elmberrow Hall and was at the back of Bredon Hill. That was enough. He set off across the fields.

One hour and three villages later he found it: a black and white timbered house with a new brick wing, set among neat shrubberies just off the lane. The Volvo, whose smell of cheroots and petrol he could pick out from a hundred metres away, was parked in a courtyard reached through an arch. The paintwork of the house was spick and span, the flowerbeds glowed with colour. The whole place looked as if lots of money had been spent on it very recently. Lucan scouted carefully around, spotted Jerry Joiner feeding plants in the orchid house, then, well satisfied, headed back for Base Camp, noting all the bends and every fork on the road.

Up in the Tower Room Lucan found the atmosphere tense. On an old newspaper was heaped a pile of sausage rolls, trifle, cold chips, egg salad, grilled bacon and pork pies which the Gang had gathered at Strensham Service Station. McKlickety was guarding it and Khamsin was in disgrace, whimpering in a corner.

'I only tried to nibble a little now so that there'd be less to carry later,' he explained, 'then they all turned on me.'

'He didn't bring a single sausage himself,' McKlickety accused, 'then he tried to wolf our snacks when we weren't looking.'

'No one likes me,' Khamsin snuffled, 'and I do try hard!'

'We all like you,' Lucan assured him, 'but you've got to try even harder.'

'Try me, boss,' Khamsin began to perk up, 'I'll do anything! Let's start now.'

'Right, but at the first sign of trouble you'll go out through the car window,' said Lucan severely. 'You can carry the raincoat. I'll take the sou'wester and gauntlets. You other four can take the food.'

In the dim drizzle they set out. The grass was very wet and they had to hold the newspaper with the snacks high to stop it getting soggy and losing the lot. But at least no one was about in the fields to see them. At the clearing they stowed the food in between the two crates of antiques, then helped Lucan into his driving gear. Sheila was put in the back. Officially she was the map reader but in fact all she did was to urge the other dogs to be careful.

'What's the order of battle, Super?' Squire asked as he settled down to his brake pedal. 'How are we going to help Ben?'

'Listen carefully,' Lucan ordered; and step by step he told them his plot.

'Geeee!' Khamsin breathed. 'That will be aggro double plus!'

'Action Stations,' Lucan called, and the Gang took to their posts.

'God bless this Moke,' said Squire, 'and all who drive in her!'

At the first turn of the ignition the Mini Moke came to life. Everyone pressed the right lever at the right time. Very slowly Lucan steered them through the overgrown entrance drive until they stood in neutral just above the hurry and swish of the motorway. It was raining again, so drivers would be keeping their eyes on the road. Lucan hitched his sou'wester into a comfortable angle, low over his furry forehead, and shrugged his mac collar up higher.

'First gear,' he called; Cassius, Khamsin and McKlickety pressed in perfect co-ordination as they began to roll.

'Second gear,' and the engine noise softened. A traffic gap was just coming up on the slow lane.

'Third,' called Lucan in triumph.

Smoothly, at just thirty miles an hour, the first dog-driven car to hit the roads of Britain moved into the southbound lane of the M5.

Still in third, not trying to overtake anything, and being overtaken themselves by several cross lorry drivers, they went up the long hill, past the Strensham Services Station and on down to the crossing of the Avon.

'We should have driven in to see Sandra and Lena for a bite of something to eat,' suggested Squire. 'That really would have surprised them.'

'It's very difficult to see where we're going with all this rain.' Lucan sounded worried.

'When my old owner drove in the rain he always pressed a button and two arms wiped the windows for him,' Squire said helpfully.

'Thanks,' said Lucan gratefully. 'It's hard to remember everything at once.'

After one misfire with the lights he got the windscreen wipers going.

'I think we can risk fourth gear,' he said. 'Stand by!'

The Moke drove even more smoothly and raised its speed to forty-five miles an hour. They even passed an old lady in a Morris 1000.

'Fourth gear is much easier on petrol,' Lucan told them knowledgeably. 'I think you can all get up now and look where we're going. Except McKlickety, of course. I'm sorry, but we do need the accelerator.'

'Talking of petrol,' said Squire, 'the tank must be almost empty. How are we going to get our five pound fifty pence worth?'

'At a self-service station,' said Lucan, 'then we won't need to speak to anyone.'

'Someone will have to pay the money at a desk and someone else will have to put the nozzle in the tank and press that lever to make the petrol flow,' Squire warned him. 'My old owner used to hate self-service because he said it made his hands smell.'

'I'm glad you've mentioned this,' said Lucan, who had, in fact, not thought his way through this particular

difficulty. 'We'll turn off here for Cheltenham and fill up while it's still raining. Then people won't notice so much.'

Only Lucan saw much of Cheltenham. Stopping and starting at traffic lights and roundabouts meant a lot of hard work. Even Sheila had to keep her nose down to the map book. A traffic jam in the High Street forced them to the left and there, in a little hollow among terrace houses, they found the perfect filling station: self-service, no cars waiting, rain pelting down.

The old gentleman at the cash window looked up from his morning paper as the Moke turned neatly in. You did not often see a Moke these days. Seemed to be a lot of dogs in it, he thought; well, everyone to their taste. A big black dog with curly hair got out. They should be kept under control. Messing about his clean petrol station, cocking their legs up on the pumps!

To his amazement, McKlickety did nothing of the sort. He reached up and stabbed the button for three star petrol, then carefully lifted the nozzle out of its socket and carried it round to the Moke's petrol tank.

Now came a pause, agonising for Lucan, interesting for the old gentleman. Inch by inch, McKlickety was unscrewing the petrol cap with his teeth.

'Help!' he called. 'The petrol nozzle is going back into the machine!'

The old gentleman saw another dog, a big white spaniel, rather dirty, step out of the Moke and stoop down beside the black dog. This was Squire taking hold of the nozzle to help McKlickety.

'Got it,' said McKlickety as the cap came off. He took the nozzle from Squire and inserted it in the tank.

'Squeeze until I tell you,' called Lucan. 'I can see how much money we're using. Don't panic. There's only one attendant and he's older than Sheila.'

This was McKlickety's most gallant moment. Just holding the heavy nozzle between his teeth had been hard, the petrol tasted harsh, cutting all interesting flavours out. But when he squeezed the lever the fumes poured into his eyes and trickles of petrol ran down his lips, burning his mouth. At 90p he had to stop a moment. Then again at £2.20, £3.45 and £4.80. This last was a long stop, his jaw was aching and his gums were burning. Lucan could see the old gentleman looking worried.

What were they doing to that black dog? Some sort of circus trick. Well, it should not be allowed. They would damage the pump. If it were not raining so hard he would go out and tell them so.

'Bring the cap in here, Squire,' Lucan ordered. 'We want to get away quickly and it will be even harder to put on. We'll do it later.'

£5.10, and McKlickety stopped again. A black Vauxhall pulled in at the next pump and a young man got out. He noticed McKlickety and smiled. Lucan turned away from him, then risked another peep at the pump gauge. It was £5.45p.

'Leave it,' he called. 'Now do your stuff, Cassius.'

The old gentleman saw the nozzle slither back on to the stand, with the black dog chasing after it. Another dog, a Boxer, was getting out now. How many more of them? And it had the money in its mouth. Slobbering all over it, no doubt.

Cassius dropped the money, rather moist, it was true, at the window.

'Here,' called the old gentleman, 'there's 5p change!'

But the dogs had all got back into the Moke and it was starting off. Funny where they had all gone to, only the driver in sight and you couldn't see much of him.

With three pips on its horn and a salvo of cheerful

barking, the Mini Moke drove off into the rain.

The young man came up to the counter.

'What d'you make of that lot?' he asked.

'Beats me,' said the old gentleman. 'They'll be driving the cars soon!'

Back in the Moke, Sheila was feeding McKlickety with salad soaked in mayonnaise because she always found it good for sore places. There was a general air of achievement.

'Any fool can drive a car,' said Lucan. 'The hard thing is getting the petrol.'

After driving three times round Cheltenham they finally found the route back to the motorway along the A40 and through Gate 11.

'Great,' said Lucan. 'Now we'll stop at Michaelwood Services to eat our snacks, drive on to Bristol, turn round at Gate 17 and come back up again to Strensham. If that policeman misses us after all that, then the police are not earning their salaries.'

At a steady forty-five miles per hour the Mini Moke, with its load of six dogs and two packing cases, set off south. The rain was clearing and the wind was rising. There was every promise of a stormy afternoon.

13
A meeting is arranged

Three hours later it was tea-time on the northbound side of Strensham Service Station. A few tattered clouds rushing furiously east dappled the brilliant sunshine. The first lorry drivers were coming in for their afternoon eat-ups at their own café, tucked away from the main building, in a corner of the car park. At one table there was deep gloom. Seated there, with three empty coffee mugs, were Fran and Julie Bosker and P.C. Malcolm Minster. They were poring over a copy of the local paper with a banner headline: 'Antique thieves foiled in raid on Stately Home', and a smaller headline: 'Gang use fierce dogs to spread chaos'. Underneath was a picture of three Dobermann dogs snarling viciously through bars at the camera. It was a very dark photograph.

Julie Bosker sucked deeply at her cigarette and blew smoke out all over the next table. Her crutch was propped against the table and she looked drawn and cross.

'It's them,' she declared. 'I'd give anything to believe it wasn't, but it's them. I'd recognise that hairy monster with hidden eyes anywhere, and that stupid long-legged beast with big ears. We've come up here on a fool's journey. They were in Worcester last night. They could be in Birmingham today.'

P.C. Minster whistled air out between his teeth and tried to look wary.

'The fact they were in Worcester last night doesn't mean they have to be in Birmingham this afternoon,' he said slowly.

'I suppose they commute on the High Speed Train, do they?' suggested Miss Julie witheringly.

'Let's say this. They're highly mobile and known to be mad on cars. At this very moment some unsuspecting lorry driver may be giving them a lift back here. The motorways have changed the whole criminal picture in this country. You can burgle a house in Carlisle and go to work next morning in Exeter.'

'We are talking about dogs, remember, not the Mafia,' Miss Julie refused to be impressed. She had suffered Fran's bad driving all the way up from Bristol to meet this policeman, and the minute they met him he had shown them newspaper photographs of her enemies in triumph. It was too much.

'Dogs are creatures of habit,' P.C. Minster declared. 'They tend to come back time and again to a den or lair. It's my belief that this den or lair is within five miles of where we're sitting now. I have based this judgement on a consideration of all known sightings of them.'

'There have only been two,' Fran pointed out.

'What I suggest,' P.C. Minster went on unperturbed, 'is that you ladies come with me in my police car to get an idea of the lie of the land in this area. You know much more about this type of animal than I do and I'm sure . . .' here he got up firmly, so that the two sisters had to do the same, though Fran had been hoping for another coffee, 'that your instinct, or shall we call it insight, will give us some lead as to an exact area for search.'

Julie Bosker hobbled awkwardly out of the café, her

forehead creased with scowl lines. P.C. Minster held the door open for both sisters and Julie stood blinking in the sunlight, squinting into it to look across the car park.

'I'll give you two hours,' she said, 'and that's generous. You're paid to do this kind of work for the community. If Fran and I hadn't had a strong sense of civic duty we'd never have come up here. Father always told us when we were children . . .'

As she had been speaking a battered little khaki vehicle, half-van and half-car, had come driving carefully off the motorway. Instead of tucking itself into the car park it made purposefully across the service area, obviously heading for the gate to the lane leading to Strensham village, where the notice read 'Exit Strictly Forbidden'. The driver was a mysteriously muffled figure, but behind him could be distinguished, through the transparent plastic flaps, the heads of several dogs. One head, Khamsin's, was hanging cheerfully out through a slit in the hood. All this grew slowly upon Julie Bosker.

'Stop me for a pig sticker,' she declared, 'if you weren't right all the time, Fran! We've got 'em!'

P.C. Minster followed her eyes and reacted like a man of action.

'Into my car,' he cried, and began to run nimbly across the car park.

'Not likely, ours is much nearer. Help me, Fran,' said Julie.

They had parked illegally, close to the Café, because of Julie's crutch; now, even with Julie's limp and Fran's fumbling of gears, their Austin Cambridge was away before P.C. Minster was into his Ford Granada. With a stately burst of middle-aged speed Fran drove out through the forbidden exit and turned left as the Mini Moke had done.

Lucan had spotted the gaudy police Granada and deliberately trailed his cape across the Service Area. Now that the bulls were after him he had his whole team at action stations. At sixty miles an hour, this particular Moke's top speed, and with McKlickety's full weight on the accelerator, they shot through Strensham village heading for Defford and the main road.

'We've missed the turn to Base Camp,' McKlickety said.

'I meant to,' Lucan told him.

They had a clear lead of two hundred metres over the Boskers and two hundred and fifty metres over the

Granada, but P.C Minster was driving like a man possessed. Twice he tried to pass the Boskers and twice oncoming traffic, combined with Fran's driving, defeated him. Finally he made it, only to see the Moke turn right at the main road, just before a stream of traffic blocked him from doing the same. He stopped abruptly, too abruptly for Fran because her Austin just grazed his bumper. He glared at her in his rear mirror and saw Miss Julie waving wildly at him. The traffic passed and he swung right, over the main railway line through Defford village. Glancing right across the fertile market gardening fields which skirt the whale back of Bredon Hill, he saw the Mini Moke across the fields, heading in almost the opposite direction on the road to Eckington. What were they playing at and who could be driving them? Was there a mysterious owner somewhere in the background? With a screech of burning tyres he threw the police car right at the Eckington turn and called up another police car to help him.

All the hedges and fields were patterned with plum and cherry blossom. Quiller Couch had written a poem about Eckington Bridge, Housman had written another poem about the 'coloured counties' around Bredon. P.C. Minster was aware of this but temporarily indifferent. Those dogs had jerked his career on to the wrong rails; somehow he felt that if he could catch up with them he would be back in the clear again. Recklessly he shot the lights at Eckington Bridge over the full flowing Avon and left his stomach suspended in mid-air by the speed with which he took the medieval hump of its arches. Now they were only fifty metres ahead. In Eckington, Lucan swung the Moke unexpectedly left at a narrow turning. P.C. Minster braked hotly, backed a metre or two, almost hitting the Bosker's Austin again, and turned left after them.

'They'll catch us this time,' McKlickety reported, looking through the rear plastic.

'If he does, we'll make him bite the bullet, and those old dames with him,' said Khamsin confidently.

'Only about a mile now to Jerry Joiner's place,' Lucan was tense with excitement over the wheel.

'But, Super, he won't help us,' said Squire.

'He won't be able to,' said Lucan grimly. 'He'll be under arrest!'

The other dogs sat trying to work that out, as they drove full-tilt out of Eckington village down a side lane. Now, with a roar of tyres on the loose surface, the Granada was up behind them and they could see the expectant smile curving on P.C. Minster's lips.

Malcolm Minster had been shown at police college how to cut in on another car and stop it. The lane was perhaps just wide enough. Gunning the engine to make a frightening noise, he drove alongside the little Moke, his right wing brushing the damson blossom from the hedge. When he was level with the driver – odd to wear a sou'wester on a fine Spring day, he thought, he looked left to make a firm gesture for them to stop.

At the self-same moment Lucan looked right and they gazed straight into each other's faces, the Bearded Collie and the policeman, both at sixty miles an hour.

P.C. Minster's jaw dropped. Something which had long been creeping quirkily at the back of his mind was suddenly, impossibly, confirmed.

It was a dog driving! They were all dogs!

Police driving instructors are first rate, but even so P.C. Minster could not quite cope with his discovery and the T-junction at the same time. His reactions were good, he braked well, but not quite well enough. Skidding broadside on, the Granada ended, with a gentle scrunch of twigs, in the hedge, while Lucan drove briskly away on the left-hand turn. The trees and roof line of Elmberrow Hall were already showing across a field of raspberry bushes and against the green loom of Bredon Hill.

Fran Bosker had only the T-junction to cope with. Unaware of the identity of the Moke's driver she edged past the stranded Granada and bustled away after Lucan. With a scurry of long-suffering tyres and a horrid scrape of ravaged paintwork, P.C. Minster pulled out of the hedge and followed her. His mind was whirling, yet he completely and immediately believed what he had just seen. It was a real dog, and it was driving a real car. The trouble was going to come when he had to convince his superior officers!

Easily ahead now, Lucan turned into the Elmberrow Hall drive, passed the shrubberies and drove through the arch into the courtyard. The Volvo was in a large open garage and Lucan drove neatly in alongside it and stopped.

'Listen, Gang,' he said. 'No questions, this is important. The police have got to find a whole heap of stolen antiques here. But the police aren't very quick and we mustn't take chances. Push over the two cases and scatter the stuff everywhere so that even he will notice it. Then out through that window and into the rhododendrons.'

Even with six big dogs pushing there was only time to topple one case out of the back, but that was enough. With a horrid crash of shattered crystal the case pitched out, the sacking flew off its top and a glittering treasure of Georgian silver, Stuart plate, Louis XIVth jewellery, Tudor miniatures and Victorian knick–knacks spilled out on to the garage floor. Gleaming dully across a heap of old lace lay the Llantyr Abbey cross, valued by Sotheby's at £180,000.

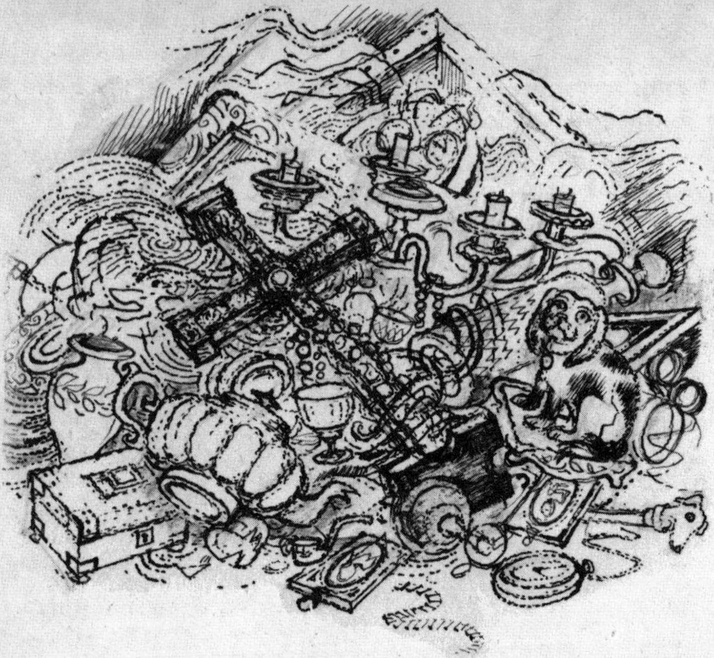

Footsteps approached across the courtyard, cars came humming up the drive.

'Good,' said Lucan, struggling out of his gloves, mac and sou'wester. 'Now let's disappear. This operation is over.'

As they came scurrying out of the Moke to leap through the rear window the solid figure of Jerry Joiner appeared in the garage door. His face was a picture of guilt as he saw all this evidence literally driven on to his doorstep, but the guilt was crossed with bewilderment as he watched Lucan shedding his gloves and the whole gang of dogs streaming out through the window. He turned to see a large black car with two angry-looking women in the front seats, obviously policewomen in civilian clothes, and behind them a police Granada with a constable in full uniform. It was a plot, it was impossible, he did not understand it, but there was no getting out of it. He was actually ankle deep in gold and silver.

P.C. Minster came leaping out of his car.

'Right, officer,' said Jerry Joiner. 'I'm making no resistance but I request my legal right to 'phone my solicitor. I take it you have a search warrant.'

The blank expressionless look which Malcolm Minster had long cultivated in the line of duty never served him better than it did at that moment.

14 The hunt goes on

The arrest of Jerry Joiner at Elmberrow Hall was only the beginning of a nine-month long investigation by the police into an antique smuggling ring all over Mid-Wales and the Midlands. But it was that first, Lucan-inspired, accidental arrest which triggered it all off. Crates of stolen silver from Swansea docks, dumps of priceless paintings in the wilds of Shropshire, they were all uncovered as a result of Lucan's firm plotting and P.C. Minster's quick-witted follow-up.

For all his mean-mindedness and dislike of animals, P.C. Minster had the makings of a brilliant policeman. Of course, he had no search warrant for Elmberrow, and of course the Bosker sisters were not policewomen. But with one fierce wink he silenced Fran and Julie; all the rest was bluff, bluff and bluff again. The other police car rolled up within five minutes, but in that brief time P.C. Minster and Fran, who was terrified and delighted by the turn of events, had marched into Jerry's office and scooped up a list of addresses which was to be the key to the whole long police investigation. They had left Jerry Joiner handcuffed to Miss Julie, which was quite enough to subdue him for five minutes.

It was an hour later, when Elmberrow was infested with police cars and Jerry Joiner was on his way to the police cells at Worcester, that Julie Bosker remembered her old enemies. She searched P.C. Minster out from a group of senior officers who were trying to discover just how he had made this tremendous breakthrough.

'What about those dogs?' she demanded. 'I suppose they're going to get off scot free, though they bust my ankle, and what's more . . .' she looked darkly around at the ravaged rooms and the five or six policemen searching the carpet with magnifying lenses, '. . . what's more, I'll bet they're behind all this!'

'What's this, Minster?' the Chief Constable had heard nothing yet of any dogs. Once more P.C. Minster's blank look came in useful:

'I believe there was a dog or two, sir, strays probably, in the back of the vehicle I'd been shadowing the last few days,' he reported. 'No trace of them since I made my arrest.'

'Nor of the driver, more's the pity, we need him,' the Chief Constable scowled. 'But I've got men out all over the area. He seems to have left most of his clothes in the garage, which is awkward for identification. I suppose you never got a good look at his face during the pursuit. Have you any idea what he looked like?'

P.C. Minster paused; the Chief Constable was very pleased with him, he would soon be offered a place at the Police Staff College in Hampshire. His career was made and he wasn't going to upset anything by telling the truth. But his nature inclined him to avoid lies, so he replied with firm conviction.

'Hairy, sir, very hairy, but I'd know him again anywhere!'